THE RUNZ GIRL

AMANDA OKPALA ADEWUSI

AMANDA OKPALA ADEWUSI

Copyright © 2021 Amanda Okpala Adewusi

All rights reserved.

AMANDA OKPALA ADEWUSI

DEDICATION

To my God in Heaven, Jesus and the holy spirit. My maker and creator who already forgave me for the sins I was yet to commit. To the Holy Spirit for saving me from situations I found myself in but couldn't explain how I got out of.

To my loving and amazing husband Peju Adewusi: From the very first day you spoke to me you ignited a flame in my heart, I just knew deep down in my heart you were the man I would spend the rest of my life with. You came into my life and changed my entire dimension of life and love and if you hadn't given your life to Christ, I couldn't imagine what my life would have been like. You have made my life worth living and I thank you.

To my beautiful baby boy Legend: My son, my pride and joy, my psychical manifestation of God, whenever I look into your eyes I'm reminded of where I'm coming from and how you saved your dad and me. You gave us hope when all odds were against us, the true meaning of love at first sight. We gave you the name Legend because you pulled us out from the pits of hell, you changed our ways completely and forced us to grow up. You broke all generational curses upon our lives, addictions and bad habits. Everything I am today is because of you; I live to make you proud you are my guardian angel.

To my mother Edith Okpala: For bringing me into this world and instilling in me the knowledge women have over men, in the 17 years

I spent with you, you taught me everything I needed to know about life, love and heartbreaks. Every day as I look at myself in the mirror, I begin to see more and more of you in me and I cannot express in words how much I miss you but I'm fully aware that you are with me and have always been with me through all my ups and downs.

To my big-headed brother Brian: You have always been by my side singing my praises to whoever was willing to listen even at times I was incapable of being the big sister you needed. I love you with all my heart, this book would not be complete without giving you Credit because you were there at the genesis of it all.

To every young girl on the path to discovering herself: I wish you success. As you read this book, I pray it keeps you focused on what's important in life and guides you into finding the light to carry you through the fire you may be experiencing. May God protect you from the things you know nothing about.

ACKNOWLEDGEMENTS

For the Mother, Daughter & Sister out there that's afraid to embrace their flaws & mistakes, this is for you.

You are beautiful, smart & flawless.

The world is yours my Queen!

CONTENTS

Acknowledgments

Introduction

1. Growing up
2. From US to Naija
3. Bankroller Ben
4. Big Time Pimping
5. The Major Heartbreak
6. Coping
7. Coming To America
8. Texas
9. Lagos!
10. P!
11. Yahoo Boys
12. Manju
13. Jezebel

To God Be The Glory!

AMANDA OKPALA ADEWUSI

INTRODUCTION

Who is a Runz Girl?

This is a question asked so many times in so many ways, but the truth is there is no one true answer because, honestly, a runz girl defies all odds. She is the girl you'd never suspect; the girl next door, your sister, your girlfriend, your wife at home, your boss at work, your banker, your assistant at work, your favourite musician or actress, your most celebrated Instagram influencer, to cut the story short, she could just be me or you. She is born from need not want.

According to the Nigerian society, there is this misconception that many runz girls are living in denial because they believe it is their right to get whatever they want all in exchange for sexual pleasures. Society has failed us in ways that are irredeemable, so in return, we have taken matters into our own hands.

It's almost like most Nigerians are operating off survival instincts and for most young beautiful women, the solution comes easy. We have been predisposed to a life of sex in exchange of some form of promise to live a better life. Who is to blame for this mindset, this hypersexualisation of the black female body? The ones who take advantage of society's preconceived expectations and judgement? The people who actually sponsor and solicit them? or the government who has offered them no alternatives?

For some women, they were forced into the lifestyle by their mothers, friends or aunts, directly and indirectly, while for others it is a generational curse. For most women in Nigeria, with little to no alternative means of making a living and a very suppressed sexual appetite due to the belief that women aren't just as much sexual creatures as their male counterparts. It's a form of escape. An escape from the harsh realities they face living in a country that says women cannot be successful without the assistance of a man. From a tender age, we are fed with fairytales of meeting our Prince Charming and getting swept off our feet with the promises of love, financial stability and security. But for most women, these promises were nothing but stories, because life tends to have its way of messing with us with things hardly working in our favour.

It's not all gloom though. As we begin to learn and unlearn certain things and open ourselves up to experience the ups and downs of life and love, we begin to form new perspectives on marriage and the female body. We are assigned who we are and what is expected of us from the moment we are born, never really giving room to understand our path and destiny, and for most of us the moment we get our chance of freedom we take it without looking back. This is what I did, I took my freedom and ran with it till I couldn't anymore. This is a book about my life, my story and my struggles, a book addressing the unspoken reality most girls like myself face growing up in a country designed to keep the average young woman on her knees, searching

for the pot of gold at the end of the rainbow. This is a raw and uncensored story of my experiences. This is my story of redemption.

Chapter 1

Growing Up

My name is Amanda Adewusi, born 4th of June 1991, in Houston Texas. I grew up in Brooklyn with my mother Edith and my little brother Brian in a little one-bedroom apartment in the heart of Flatbush. Our life was a simple yet complicated life. We didn't alot but we had enough for each other.

I lived most of my childhood in Brooklyn. The memories are still fresh, it feels just like yesterday. I remember walking through the front doors and the smell of cigarettes instantly welcoming me, rap music booming through the first-floor hallway and the usual sound of kids echoing through the walls. There was always something going on in that building and my mom always made sure we never had anything to do with it. Drug dealers doing what they did best Couples arguing, people gambling, and gang bangers posted up alongside the building, you never really knew what was going down and when it was going down.

It was not the best environment, but it was home to us. Most times we had to take the stairs to make it up to our apartment due to the lack of maintenance; something was always falling. For a one-bedroom New York apartment, ours was surprisingly big, big enough to fit each of us comfortably. We had this massive king-sized bed and all three of us slept in it every night comfortably. I grew up watching my mother hustle two jobs and still give us 100% attention. She never missed a PTA meeting, or a school dance or play and she was always early to pick us up. For the most part, she didn't own a car so we took the bus and train a lot and that was fine with us. We loved it, it was fun!

My mother was as much American as she was Nigerian. When I tell you she was with the shits, believe me. She was a firecracker, a ticking time bomb but at the same time, she was the life of the party, a sweetheart. Anywhere "Edith Amakwe" walked into she lit up. Standing at about 6 feet tall she commanded so much attention when she walked into any room, I mean you just couldn't miss her. Always in the latest fashion accessories and is never scared to flaunt her killer curves. Honestly, if I had to choose someone to be my mother I would choose her over and over again.

I remember every birthday we spent at Chuck E Cheese, every trip to Toys R Us where we got to choose any toy in the store and she would pay for it, I remember every Friday was pizza night and we got to go to bed late. Some kids grew up with memories of flying private jets and touring different countries, while we did nothing of such we had pretty awesome memories. How many kids can say they spent their summer holidays selling ice cream out of Mr Softee ice cream trucks and making money? We had unique memories. Driving down Flatbush avenue in a freezing truck with access to all the ice cream flavours you could think of and all the loose change and dollar bills laying carelessly around his truck.

My mother had two sides to her, when she wasn't being so mean she was making sure we grew up lacking nothing and when I mean nothing she made sure she provided. We never lacked anything or ever felt inadequate amongst our peers. My mother was a hustler and a provider. She did what needed to be done and we never saw her break a sweat. She worked in the city as a social worker and at the time we didn't know what she did but we knew it had something to do with being nice to kids. We would follow her to her work events and sit there upset because we would rather be home watching tv but here we were being dragged to work. She made sure she kept us busy on Saturdays and we hated it. Anyone who ever met my mom would say she was the sweetest person ever, well how can someone so sweet be so brutal? hahaha.

Brutal? You ask, yup! My mom was one tough cookie and I never understood why she was so hard on me. It was like nothing I ever did could satisfy her. She was just so damn angry. I never could put my finger on it and I wondered " *does she think I'm gonna get pregnant and get caught up in these Brooklyn streets, what does she take me for?, who does she think I am?*".

My mom and I had a toxic relationship because I was equally a stubborn child. I broke rules, constantly got into trouble at school. I never wanted to be in class so I constantly made it a point of duty to disrupt classes. Could that have been the reason for my mother's harshness towards me? maybe. On the other hand, my body was developing fast and considering the kind of neighbourhood we lived in I was like fresh meat being dangled in a den of lions. She was extremely overprotective of me and didn't want to leave room to chance. She would slap, kick, punch, push or throw something or wrestle me to the ground when I did anything wrong. She used different things at different times, it was either wires, belts, or shoes.

At some point, I contemplated running away. There was a time I secretly packed my bags but the thought of how I would survive in the streets and shamelessly come back home to beg for forgiveness because I couldn't survive on my own deterred me from going through with the plans. As the child I was I had no choice but to endure it all and wait till I was old enough to leave and never come back. Despite it all, I loved my mom to death, but those occasional beatings had me questioning her love for me. Because of her fear of me going wayward and joining the ways of the street, I wasn't allowed to hang out with my friends, go to the park, talk on the phone, talk to boys. I wasn't allowed to do the things other teenagers had the privilege of doing. My life outside school was boring, so I made sure I had the most fun in school. People would say I was quite popular and so were my friends. We were the hottest, flyest girls in our grade and we had all the boys flocking around us.

Back at home, my life was different. I had more pedigree in school than at home. As the overprotective mother that she was, she didn't take us for granted. Brian, my little knucklehead brother, had it so easy growing up. I envied him. She spoiled him. People sometimes commented that my mum spoiled me a lot. Now imagine when I say she spoiled Brian. Whatever sweet thing she did for me, she did ten times more than that for Brian, her golden child. He did no wrong in her book, everything Brian wanted he got and that drove me insane.

Brian and I would get into fights a lot because I hated his guts. I hated the fact he knew he was my mother's favourite and never hesitated to rub it in my face. He tormented me and had fun with it. I gave him the nickname "knucklehead" and still call him that till now. As much as he was a knucklehead, I couldn't love him any less.

Seeing him made him happy and the memories of our fights bring smiles to my face.

Our life was pretty awesome courtesy of Uncle Chris. He was a family friend and the only thing I remember about him was his filthy lifestyle whew! For some reason we always got dumped off at Uncle Chris' and to be honest he didn't really appreciate the babysitting duties, but he had no choice. Uncle Chris was a tall dark-skinned man, in his late thirties, out of shape and always had his potbelly hanging out and his butt crack showing. Facially he was handsome but, in his case, looks didn't cut it. He lived a couple of blocks down the street from us in this disheveled apartment complex that was everything short of clean. He lived in a tiny and filthy one-bedroom apartment, it was dark and dingy with rats and roaches - the big New York City roaches (those roaches are built differently). He lived with those roaches like it was nothing! They were everywhere; just crawling around freely and he never cared. He would even joke about them being his family and friends. It made me sick, sick to my stomach. I always wondered how a full-grown man could function in such a grim environment. I mean this man was a mess! But how my mother could dump us there all the time had me even more confused. I guess when you have to work and don't have money for babysitters you gotta do what you gotta do right?

One thing about Uncle Chris is he always kept a stack of quarters and dollar bills laying around. Asides from the roaches and rats you were stepping on; the place was littered with dollar bills and coins in every denomination you could think of. It was like a trap house full of money, and I was always there to steal 'em. Anytime we were getting dumped over I made sure I was prepared to steal money. I would easily walk out of

his apartment with ten to fifteen dollars in cash and some change and he wouldn't notice. At that time and considering my age it was a huge amount of money. I could buy all the pizza slices I wanted, I could flex in school, I could buy a cute doll or some fake press on nails. I stole whatever I knew could get me what I wanted and ensured I didn't get caught. His place was my nightmare and piggy bank at the same time!

Uncle Chris was doing pretty well for himself I would say, but he was a cheapskate, he didn't spend anything on himself at all you could tell just by looking at him and visiting his apartment. Nonetheless, he had a nice car, an ice cream truck business that was racking in so much money during the summer holidays and he always kept himself a girlfriend. I wondered how he was able to attract any woman? He always had girls flocking around him. Anytime we came over they would either be preparing to leave or heading to work, and I would sit there so confused wondering how any normal functioning woman could lay with this man in this cesspool of filth or even kiss this man.

I never failed to give them a disgusting look anytime I saw them, especially when they kissed him goodbye.

Later on, when I learnt the word gold-diggers, it all made sense. One week they were all loved up, cooking and laying with him in his crummy apartment. The next week he's explaining to someone on the phone (most times my mother) why and how they broke up, stole from him, or finessed him out of hundreds of dollars. I was young but not stupid; it was not hard to figure out they only wanted his money. Wondering why he didn't figure that out.

Summer holidays were always the best. We had sleepovers, late nights, carnivals and the best part of it all, our cousins in Nigeria always came to visit. See, they were rich! They lived the life we knew nothing about. To me, they had it all. One thing I could never really understand was why anytime they came into the country they had to stay with us, in that one-bedroom apartment where the three of us were barely managing. Although it was huge, it was only huge for three people. With seven people, it became incredibly small. Nonetheless, we got to spend our summer holidays showing them life in the big city, the fast life, the hustle and bustle and the ghetto we called Brooklyn. They loved it, we loved it, life was fun. Summers always went by quickly especially when it's filled with fun but saying goodbyes were always the hardest thing to do and life would return to its boring self after they left. The cycle starts all over again.

Chapter 2

From the US to Naija!

I was 11 years old when my mother decided we were going to move back to Nigeria to become a family and when I say family, I mean it in the loosest way possible. My dad had decided suddenly, after years of abandonment, to involve himself in our lives. Selfishly disregarding the damages and gap he had left when he chose himself over his family. My mom, whom I think could no longer handle the pressure of taking care of 2 children with little to no support in a foreign country, uprooted our lives and went back to that man. So, one day we packed up what we knew as our lives and moved across the world to Africa, Nigeria to be precise.

I remember my first moments. As the plane landed and I looked out of the window, everything felt strange. It didn't look like where we were coming from. Everything down to the smell of the place was different, I can clearly remember the unadulterated dread that sank into my stomach as we rushed around the Murtala Muhammed Airport. I thought to myself, *"where on earth are we? where the hell did mommy bring us to? What the hell is going on out here?"*. The blazing cruel and unwelcoming sun that greeted us alone as we stepped out of the plane was enough to deter our entire experience. From day one, upon landing I was livid!

"*My daughter*", a voice says from behind.

I turned to look at the person speaking and was greeted with a tight suffocating hug. *Who is this man? And why the hell was he touching me?*

The same person turned to pick my brother off the ground when my mother whispered to my confused self, *"that is your daddy"*.

My Daddy, somehow that had no impact on me.

My initial response was "*oh nice*" as I continued to look around at the faces that had now become my reality? The bittersweet feeling of now having a father present was something I just couldn't shake off, to be honest. I didn't care for his presence, it made no difference in my life, it was like he was there, but he wasn't there.

For the next couple of years, we lived in Nigeria. My father tried the best way he could, I'm sure, to step up and fill the void, but to us, there was never really a void, our mother was always all we needed and no one else. He was just an extra, an extra we didn't care for. We didn't care for him and no matter how much he tried, he was pushed farther away, it just didn't feel right.

It broke his heart that he was invisible to us and that led to numerous arguments between my parents. Some nights, things would escalate to physical fights and furniture would be tossed around. My mom would always try to bribe us to make him feel fatherly but how was it possible? I was old enough to understand his absence and I was comfortable with it. It is hard for anyone to accept a new reality after 11 years, especially when you are expected to accept this reality in such a short time. His inability to understand this made life tense for all of us.

To shorten the distance between us, our father thought the best way to get the love he demanded out of us was to forcefully coerce us to refer to him as "daddy". So, he would say things like, "*before I give any of you money in this house you must call me daddy, address me as your father*". And because of how distasteful those words sounded coming out of our mouths, it only drove the wedge between us further away. I have memories of my brother and me standing outside his door for hours debating on who would take the bold step into his room and say, "*daddy can we...?*"

The asking part was never the issue, it was always the "daddy" part for us, it just never felt right. Never had a word sounded so wrong and thick down my throat.

On top of not being a good dad, my father was also not a good husband. He was a serial cheater and didn't care one bit for my mom's feelings. I saw all of this, and it only made me hate him more. I just couldn't find a place in my heart to accommodate him. I remember the first time I caught him cheating on my mom. I remember it like it was yesterday. Janice was a girl in my neighborhood. I had always referred to her affectionately as my school mom even though she wasn't in my school, but I considered her my school mom because she was slightly older than me, a couple of classes above me and we lived on the same street, just a few houses apart.

I was walking down to my friend's house one day, after school. And behold, my dad's car pulled up around the corner, we locked eyes, all three of us.

Why was Janice in the front seat of my dad's car? Why were they driving past her house even if he was dropping her off at home? How the hell do they even know each other?

These questions plagued my mind as I continued strolling down the street in a rage, then a light bulb came on in my head, *could Janice be dating my dad? Is that why she's nice to me? Has she been using me to get close to my dad this entire time?*

"Wow!" I thought bitterly.

I brushed it off because part of me still wanted to be friends with her. I mean, she was gorgeous, stood at about 6 feet tall and when she smiled, it honestly was like she lit up an entire room, there was just something about her personality that was unshakeable. Seeing her with my dad, all I could think was she deserved better!

Crazy right? Before you start to judge me, I couldn't hold her responsible for the whole affair. He was my father, after all, a married, middle-aged man fraternising with a teenager, he should have known better. Clearly, he didn't. It was apparent to me, even at that age that, if she was with my dad, she needed something, and it was definitely not love, well at least it seemed like that to me.

Just like that, the dislike I had for my father grew even stronger. No longer passive, it seemed to all like it was overnight. The awkwardness and tension grew even thicker; to him, I probably seemed like just a child, a silly child, but to me, he was a no-good cheat and it pissed me off to my very core knowing that we were bundled down to this country to start a life with this man. At this point, I was done with pretending. I had absolutely no reason to even try to build a relationship with this man that may have been my biological sperm donor but meant nothing to me. It was what it was.

For some obscure reason, I kept this secret, and it was like he knew I would right from the moment we locked eyes. I hated doing so but I felt like I didn't have a choice. It was never addressed, and I never brought it up, this was because of how much I loved my mom but knew also how much of a wild card she could be. I refused to tell her. You see my mom was sweet and gentle, but she was also a maniac. My mother played no games, and she was ready to put hands on whoever messed with her, so part of me always shielded her from the truth out of the fear of putting her in a situation where she would act out of character.

So, it's safe to say in this case I was protecting my dad and Janice from the wrath of my mother.

This was not how my father saw it though. It was like that one secret kept untold turned into a silent bond. My father must have thought we shared some kind of truce or pact because what had seemed to be a one-time thing had now turned into me catching him flirting with girls shamelessly or exchanging numbers.

It truly made me sick to my stomach, I couldn't, for the life of me, understand what my mother and every other woman saw in him. I couldn't understand why they got married talk less of staying married. I couldn't understand how girls could openly exchange numbers with a man with two kids right in front of them: such disrespect!

My father was my first introduction to a cheating Nigerian man. His friends weren't any better either. As the saying goes, truly birds of a feather flock together.

Yuck!

Every time he brought me around them for whatever reason, I could feel them undressing me with their eyes. From the ones who leaned in for too long hugs to not so subtly and perversely feel my breast graze upon their perverted chests, to the ones with the inappropriate "compliments" and lines of questions.

Yup, I was aware too. Unfortunately, I grew up too fast due to past situations and traumas I had faced separate from him in my short life, I knew all the signs and tricks. So, every time they leaned in for one of those dreadful and revolting hugs; guess what I did?

Gave them the church hug. You know the hug from the side; the one where instead of your breast pushing up on their chest it's your shoulder. Obviously, they hated it but they got it every single time unfailingly. What type of man would sit there and sexualize their friend's underage daughter? I'll tell you, Nigerian men!

My first introduction to having a father was the most disappointing, heartbreaking, and most disillusioning experience. I was never really hungry for a father figure, nor did I crave the presence of a man in my family because I had all I needed- my loving mother, my baby brother and a good enough life. The fact that I was catered off to a new country that looked completely different from where I was used to made me angry. I loved my mum and still do but I felt like she took us from the pot to the fire and I was forced to live with the depressing realisation that my family and my mother's happiness was literally in my hands, yet I couldn't tell anyone, and I was forced to live with the antagonist of my story.

Chapter 3

Bankroller Ben

Nigeria was a new territory for me. It felt like I left the desert for the jungle in a sense. New threats and worries. Walking down my street, as a young teenager, alone was always a recipe for disaster. From men stopping to wave me down and catcalling inappropriate nicknames and "endearments" to the ones following behind me, stalking closely, with promises of changing my life. It was very bemusing, to say the least.

I mean sheesh I was only 15, I didn't need my life changed. I was very content with the way my life was, and from my experience of change, I understood it wasn't always for the better.

Not all of them were paedophiles though. I was a well-developed child; some men may have guessed my age was higher than it actually was because I was slightly overdeveloped and looked a lot more mature than I actually was. I hit puberty at a really young age, so my body took shape early on and my curves came in quickly. Also, because my family was plagued with the big breast syndrome, I was cursed with carrying around breasts bigger than my young body could manage.

Not only was it a major distraction to most boys I interacted with, but it also caused me major back pain at a young age. At that age, the size of my breasts made me very insecure. I felt it was the first thing that stuck out about me, and it put me in a lot of awkward positions, positions I had no business being in at that age. I wasn't alone though. I found someone I could relate to and luckily, she became my friend. Her name was Maria, she lived on the opposite end of my street, and she was just like me it seemed, and people would always confuse us for sisters, so we bonded almost instantly.

Maria had lived in Lagos almost all her life, she moved there when she was younger, so she was used to everything Lagos threw at her including men's inappropriate advances. I was a year older than her, but she looked and acted way older than I did because her body was way more developed and shapelier than mine was. Not only that though, but she was also doing something I had not even considered myself old enough to talk about without blushing; she had been having sex, a lot of sex.

Yes, Maria was a fast girl, she was going 95mph in a 50-mph zone if you get what I mean. Nonetheless, I liked her. She showed me the ropes. Even though I was a virgin, and she wasn't, there was never any judgement between us, just understanding. In fact, I was eager to learn from her, I needed her expertise on how to navigate this new stage of my life where I was becoming more aware of the opposite sex and vice versa. I didn't even know what to do with a boyfriend let alone a couple of them!

At that age, she was already experienced with the business of men and how to juggle them all at 14 years old!

I came to learn that not only was her mother fully aware of her sexcapades, but she was also in full support of them as well. She needed the money Maria was bringing home from these admirers of hers and was willing to turn a blind eye to it all. It was almost like she was pimping her daughter out to the highest bidder or shall I say, bidders. Every day was like a revolving door at her house; I would watch different men pull up to her gate with cash gifts, food or new clothes and to be honest it made me a bit jealous because she was younger than me yet she was much more advanced and experienced than I was, and here I was, completely dependent on my mommy for the smallest things and debating with my brother on whose turn it was to go ask for money from the sperm donor. Here was Maria, on the other hand, cursing these men out because they didn't bring her the right plate of food or the money, they gave her wasn't enough for what she wanted. I was blown away by her audacity. The confidence in her voice and attitude when she spoke to these men left me utterly in awe and flabbergasted.

I wanted to be just like her; I wanted the audacity to speak to men in a derogatory manner if they didn't heed to my immediate demands. I wanted them to worship me the way they worshipped her, and she always made sure to rub it in how she had them eating out the palms of her hand. I was also jealous and yearning for the freedom she seemed to have, and how she seemed to have it all figured out. I was jealous of a lot of things -her self-confidence- something I lacked at that stage in my life, her upbringing- as unconventional as it was, and most of all her body. She stood tall with those heavy breasts that made me slouch and carried them with grace no matter how heavy it seemed to look. I wanted to be like her, but I couldn't summon the confidence.

As it turned out, I was also attracting the attention of some of these men just by being around Maria. It was new and scary. I was always the shy one, some went as far as calling me anti-social, I was the introverted one in the friendship. I never really cared to be noticed, especially not by men because I had been through some traumatic experiences in the hands of men and that made me self-conscious and cautious around them but hanging around Maria got me all the wrong attention. Now as men came to see her, they would be sure to bring a friend for me as well because we were always together, all the time, well at least when she was home from school. After all, Maria attended a boarding school and was only home during the holidays.

Everywhere Maria was, I was right there, right beside her, observing everything. Slowly I started opening up to the advances of men. There we were, a 14 and 15-year-old girl hanging out with guys in their late 20s, going on dates and getting gifts. It was so bad I couldn't even bring these gifts home because there was nowhere, I could put them without my mom stumbling onto them. So, most times I left them at Maria's, other times I would give them away.

It wasn't too long, we became notorious. I mean we were never just at home innocently doing things girls our age at that time did, always on the prowl! You would catch us eating out at all the little fast-food restaurants in the area, sitting in the front seats of different Mercedes Benz with men twice our ages and shopping for shit we didn't even need.

I remember the first day I saw Maria with a man, he had a full beard, a ton of jewellery on and his own car, there was no way the guy was old, he looked no less than 30 years old. Maria called him Tony and introduced him as her boyfriend and as he came out of his car, they shared a passionate kiss right there in the middle of the street. I was blown away that it was such a bold thing, I couldn't have imagined myself kissing a man so boldly and passionately right in front of my gate. My mother would have buried me right there and then but that was Maria's freedom she could do anything she wanted with anyone she wanted to. Tony had brought a friend whose name was Elvis, slightly shorter than Tony but they dressed alike, and he introduced Elvis as his best friend. As we all walked back into Maria's house, I watched the two of them fondle each other openly without a care in the world. I craved that kind of affection, and I couldn't wait to find a boy I could do stuff like that with. As we sat inside watching TV Maria and Tony excused themselves and left Elvis and me alone in the living room, so we began talking. He asked me questions about myself, and I did the same and one thing led to another he had me laughing and blushing at the same time.

Elvis seemed like a cool guy, and I was willing to explore further so we exchanged numbers as we waited for Maria and Tony to return from the room. As they returned, I noticed how scruffy they were looking, and Maria had a look of guilt written all over her face while Tony smiled from ear to ear. They didn't have to say much. It was obvious what had just gone down, Elvis and I looked at each other and started laughing. Tony decided we all should go out to eat, so we hopped in the back of his car and went along for the ride. Elvis had been a gentleman the entire night and as they dropped me off at home, I gave him a kiss on the cheek and told him goodnight.

We began talking and texting each other a lot more and he would come to see me from time to time while I was at Maria's house.

One day on my stroll to Maria's as I approached the gate, I saw a big black Cadillac Escalade parked outside. This car was the definition of sexy, I had never seen anything like it before, matte bodywork, fully tinted, and some shiny rims. Who the hell could this be? Who has Maria caught this time? This one seems like a big fish o. These were my thoughts as I walked towards the house. I was so eager to get inside that I tripped over myself. As I walked into the gate, all I could hear was laughter. As I entered the house, I saw all of them seated, her mom and this big, dominating, tall, dark-skinned man with a gold tooth and a bunch of gold jewellery around his neck and on his fingers with Maria positioned like a cute baby on his lap. Everything about him screamed rich! He reminded me of those 80's old school hood pimps in the black American hood classic movies; those ones that sold drugs and pimped out women. He looked the part to the T! I grew up watching those movies, but this felt surreal quite honestly and to be honest I was intrigued. Immediately I walked in and greeted everyone as casually as I could without giving away my curiosity and anxiety. Maria got up, ran over to me and pulled me closer, almost childlike, (like a little girl would to her shy friend), to him and said, "Amanda meet my favourite uncle Ben".

This was strange because she had never introduced any of her previous men to me as uncle nor had I ever seen any of them in her house sitting down comfortably so I assumed he had to have been related to her as this gathering seemed personal. As I politely greeted him, he grabbed my hand and held it tight, pulling me closer a little and said with a wicked smile on his face "oh so you're the Amanda I have been hearing about".

With a confident smirk of my own, even though deep down I felt none of the confidence I displayed, I answered "yes I am."

"Lovely", he responded.

It was then Maria interjected and playfully said "Ben, you too like women, please leave my friend alone!" And I thought "Woah!" He must be the coolest uncle ever as I had never had any interactions with my uncles like that.

Ben stood up to leave and dipped his hands in his pockets and brought out the first bundle of money like it was a mere stack of paper and tossed it over to Maria's mom. She exclaimed in gratitude and began to hail him. Then once again he dipped his hand back in his pocket, brought out the second bundle of cash and tossed it at Maria, the exclamation of hails and gratitude continued. Just when I thought it was over, he once again dipped his hand in his pocket and tossed another bundle of cash at me. I couldn't help but stare at both the money in my hand and the man who threw it at me in awe and shock.

Who was this guy exactly?

How deep were his pockets? Both figuratively and literally?

These questions ran through my mind as I stood there. It wasn't new to me, getting money from men but this was different. We had been getting money here and there from men we had previously entertained, but it was a chicken change compared to what Ben had thrown at us all in a short period of time. Right then and there I knew who I wanted... scratch that needed as a boyfriend! It was Ben, I was attracted to the power, the sheer audacity and the money obviously. It was suddenly like I had graduated from moving around with 20 somethings with chicken change to give and petty trinkets of affection to full-grown men with deep pockets.

It had to be Ben.

The question though, after this sudden realisation was how I was going to pull that off?

I didn't know where to start. I didn't know the rules, the unspoken ones at least when it came to family. I didn't want to seem like I was coming after a family member especially after I heard them ask about his wife, he was a family man so this was new territory for me.

Were family members off-limits? I didn't know the rules that governed this game and had never thought to even ask. But the way he had held my hand earlier… I knew there was something there and I was willing and ready to explore.

As we walked Ben back to his car, each of us with a smile on our faces, he asked if he could come back the next day to take us to lunch.

"Yes!", I excitedly blurted out. Realizing how jumpy I had been, I cringed immediately, "I mean why not!" I said trying to sound a bit more casual this time.

Maria, on the other hand, was not too pleased about the excitement in my voice and my general reaction to her uncle. Her mood darkened almost immediately, and she became irritated and moody. As we walked back to the house after watching him drive off with our hands in the air waving, I already knew I needed to start damage control.

"Dang!" I thought to myself, "Amanda you were way too forward, family must definitely be off-limits".

Before I could get a word in, Maria turned to me with a glare on her face, it did nothing to mask the jealous expression she wore underneath it.

"So, you like him eh?" she said in a voice that had a hint of venom in it

"Me ke, No o. How will I like your uncle?" I immediately denied it!

"I was just excited about the money he gave us! It's so much!" I said trying to cover up, hoping she believed me. My face was neutral and innocent. She must have believed me because an arrogant grin burst through as she said to me "Oh that?"

She laughed. "That's chicken change compared to what he usually gives me", she said as we walked back into the house. After that, we conversed and chatted like we normally would. I let out a secret sigh of relief that she suspected nothing.

Hmm!

As I got home later that night from Maria's, the thought of seeing Ben again excited me. I couldn't sleep. I literally counted down the hours to our next meet up with him. It was my childlike mind's version of a crush I guess but for some reason, I couldn't help but feel like Maria was going to sabotage our meet up plans on purpose because of what happened the day before.

The D-day came, the day I was to see Ben again. I was super excited; I almost couldn't control it. As I got dressed, I remembered Maria's reaction the day before. It was strange but I guess she is just being jealous, maybe a little. But why would she be jealous if he was truly her uncle. I still didn't know what the rules are but since she is not saying anything, I am going to assume there are no rules. All these thoughts plagued my mind as I continued to get ready and tried my best to look cute. I stared in the mirror after, taking in myself. Suddenly I remembered my reaction from yesterday and I felt like pounding my head against a wall.

Stupid!

How dumb I was! I had shown my hand and now, if Maria could help it, I would probably never be in the same room with her Uncle Ben again.

Well, whatever! I said, shaking the thought off. I'm still going to look cute and go over there and that's exactly what I did. As I got there Maria was dressed too and thirty minutes later Ben showed up in his nice ostentatious car, he honked three times outside and we rushed outside to meet him.

I guess she must have forgiven me for my little outburst yesterday.

"whew thank God!" I let out under my breath as we ran outside to meet him. She jumped in the front seat riding shotgun as I gently slid into the back seat and scooted over to the back of the passenger seat. This was perfect because I wanted to get a good look at this man without Maria catching me. The interior of this car was very luxurious; it had beige leather seats, and tv screens in the back and on the dashboard and I must say it smelled nice too, of perfume and rich leather. This guy was smooth, he knew all the right things to say and do and slowly he had checked off my entire checklist. "This was going to be my first Sugar daddy!" I thought to myself with a renewed determination.

"So where would you like me to take you ladies?" he asked as he drove out. "Anywhere nice and expensive" Maria answered. I knew I couldn't go too far because I needed to be available and reachable if my mom called and asked; I needed to be able to get my ass back home and fast! So, I insisted on Chicken Republic. Not exactly the luxury I was seeking but it had to do. Now at this time, the fast-food chain was quite new and had just opened. I knew a lot of people who had raved about the chicken and fries and anyone who knew me knew I loved me some french fries.

On our way to Chicken Republic, the weirdest thing happened in the car and to be honest I was appalled. When we first got in the car he was playing music and we got to watch the actual videos playing on the screen throughout the entire car but halfway through the drive, he said: "let me put something that will blow your minds".

And just like that, he switched the CD to what I could never have guessed he would have for the life of me. Actual porn started playing on every screen.

"Woah! What the actual hell is going on?!" I thought as my eyes widened in sheer shock. I don't think I had ever seen porn before then. My jaw dropped and I became agitated. I looked over at Maria, but to my surprise, she was totally fine with it. her eyes were glued to that screen while he laughed and called her bad girl.

"Isn't this your uncle?" I thought in panic. What kind of sick perverted uncle is this?

The mere thought put a sour taste in my mouth, I became extremely uncomfortable, but I couldn't do anything about it. Maira wasn't complaining and I certainly wasn't going to say anything if she didn't, so we rode like that to the restaurant with the sounds of moans and grunts from the porn echoing loudly in the car.

Finally, we got to the restaurant, and I was relieved. I thought that was the end of the abuse to my senses, but I was very sadly mistaken. As we sat in the restaurant waiting for our food, the events that took place began to rub me the wrong way (no pun intended). We sat in a booth, and I sat across from both of them, and although they were openly flirting in front of me, I didn't even care. What utterly shocked me to my core was that this man had his hand up her skirt and he wanted me to know too. He made it as obvious as possible, from my perspective, he fingered his niece in front of her best friend in a public fast-food joint all the while making eye contact with me. At this point, I couldn't believe what I was seeing and so many questions were running through my mind.

Is this man really her uncle or did she just say that to me because he was off-limits? Could he really be her uncle and her mom doesn't know they are having sexual relations? Or maybe she does?

Hmm! Was I meant to continue believing the lie that he was her uncle and forget everything happening in front of me? Whew, it was too much to take in, my brain was in overdrive. As they finished up, the waiter brought our food, and we ate as if nothing had happened.

As we finished up and headed back into the car a conversation ensued. A conversation about Maria wanting to follow Ben and his girls on their next trip to Italy, and every time she brought it up, he would shut her down and let her know her mother would not hear of it, but Maria continued pleading. I wanted to go to Italy too. Even though I had no idea what was going on in Italy, I just knew that if he was going to take Maria, then I was coming along as well.

At some point during the ride, Maria requested to stop at a pharmacy and pick up something for her mom, so Ben reached into his pocket, brought out a wad of cash (which, at this point, I realised he never just carried singles) and handed it to her as she hurried into the store. So here we were, I was still not deterred from my plan to get him as my sugar daddy despite what had gone down. We were alone in the car and trust me to make my move.

"So what's happening in Italy? Whatever it is, I want to come too" I said, trying to be cute for him.

He turned to me and, with a smile, said "I own a modelling agency of a sort. It's very prestigious. I fly girls over there to model abroad and live as well" This caught my attention immediately.

An escape from my crappy life. That was what he sounded like he was offering me. I scooted closer to him in excitement and told him all about my modelling dreams and how I've always wanted to become one and how my huge breasts are not exactly conducive for the petite dresses models got to wear, if it wasn't for it, I could have passed for a model.

With a smirk on his face, he said "of course you're already a model, that's why I can't take my eyes off you. You're so sexy! I think you could even become a superstar. You have an American passport, right?"

"Yes", I eagerly replied.

"Great," he said, "it would make my job so much easier."

At this point, I knew nothing, not even my friendship with Maria could stand in my way of getting this guy. He was my lifeline and my getaway plan, my escape from this God-forsaken country Nigeria (As I used to think of it then). Oh, how I hated Nigeria, so many days I thought of running to the American embassy and asking them to get me outta there, but I knew it would come at a price; the price of being taken away from my mother and brother so I counted my days down and said once I was turned eighteen, I was getting on a plane and saying adios.

Ben pulled out a piece of paper and wrote his number down and placed it in my hand and said "Call me when you're home and alone. Let's discuss how we can fit you into my next batch of girls, but make sure you don't tell your friend, or she's going to get very jealous." He didn't have to tell me that twice as I stuffed the paper into my bra, readjusted back into my seat and sat there with a big smile on my face as Maria climbed back into the car and we headed back home. When we got back to the house, I jumped down out of the car excited waiting to go in with Maria but I noticed I was the only one out of the car. I figured she might want to have alone time with him, so I gave them their space to talk while I walked into the house to wait for her. No rush, I already got what I needed, and it was just a matter of time before I would be running home to make my million-dollar phone call.

As evening approached, I got up to leave Maria's house. I had never been in such a hurry to get home. I literally ran home, went straight up to my room and into my bed, pulled out his number from my bra and called him. It rang once and was immediately disconnected so I decided to text, "Hi this is Amanda, Maria's friend." and almost immediately he called me back. We were on the phone for about thirty minutes and just like that Ben became my first sugar daddy.

We spoke on the phone every single day multiple times a day. At a point, I had to change his name on my phone so Maria wouldn't know it was him. I also had to constantly delete our chat history just to keep us a secret and it ate me up inside because I lived with the fear of her finding out and it turning ugly.

On my first date with Ben, he sent me an address and asked me to take a taxi to come to see him. When I showed up, he sent someone down to pay the taxi and escort me up. Such a gentleman I thought, the other guys I had been with became little boys to me now that I have started dealing with a grown man. As I entered the room to what I had figured to be a guest house, I saw him talking on the phone, shirtless with a bulging tummy and pants sagging. It wasn't a cute sight, to be honest, but what caught my attention was the pile of naira notes carelessly scattered on the table beside him and the bundle of hundred dollar bills right beside it. Now that's what I was talking about foreign currency baby! As he rounded up his phone call and threw his phone on the bed he yelled "now my baby is here I can relax" and made his way over to me and hugged me tight, pressing my chest tightly to his. No, I didn't give him the church hug; he was my sugar daddy not my uncle he leaned in and planted a juicy kiss on my lips and I almost threw up, it was beyond disgusting.

As much as I planned and plotted for him, you would have thought

I liked him, ha-ha nope he was a raggedy, perverted 40 something-year-old married man with a potbelly, what could I have possibly wanted him from except his resources duh! He poured me a glass of Hennessy which I rejected. Because first I was underage and wasn't used to alcohol. Second, I was kind of scared of the adverse reaction it would have on me. In short, I didn't want to end up going home drunk out of my mind, but of course, he forced me to take a couple of sips which I did, and it was disgusting but I drank it anyway. As he hopped on the bed he shifted over and asked me to join him. My heart was beating in milliseconds, Amanda if this man rapes you who are you going to tell? How are you going to ever forgive yourself? Are you ready to lose your virginity to this creep? Hell no was my answer and I immediately mentally prepared myself for an escape plan, and one thing Amanda always knew how to do was get ready for an ugly scenario. I had been in way too many to not be prepared when the situation arose (more on this later).

I sat on the bed beside him still holding my glass of Hennessey pretending to be sipping it when it was only grazing the top of my lip. He grabbed my thigh then boom! His phone rang "whew saved by the bell." Ben's phone rang nonstop. I mean he seemed to be a busy man by the way his phones rang, how he managed to always be laid up in different rooms confused me. After this call he plopped back on the bed and began caressing my leg and immediately I pulled away he said, "don't be scared I don't bite" I giggled and replied, "I'm a virgin and I'm not having sex with you!" he seemed surprised and even doubted me, but I assured him I was and said he could stylishly ask his niece girlfriend Maria. He laughed, shrugged it off and said "wow! Now I love you more, I'm going to spoil you, I'm going to make you my second wife, I'm going to be the one to dis-virgin you." I thought to myself "how sickening.

We spent the next hour or so talking and getting to know each other. By 6 pm it was time for me to head home so he called his boy to get me a taxi and again handed me a wad of cash and a hundred-dollar bill, then said no you deserve more and made it three hundred dollars. Wow, I was amazed, little ole me walking out of there with three hundred dollars and a whole lot of naira that couldn't even fit in my pockets, so he wrapped it in a couple of plastic bags, and I hurried home.

The next couple of days I felt untouchable, I had so much money hidden in the back of my closet I didn't know what to do with it or what to spend it on and I damn sure didn't own a bank account. The most I did was take the money to school, flex and buy a whole bunch of food and snacks for me and my girls. I started dating this boy in school, Thomas Alabi. He was the school's biggest playboy, this boy had all the girls crushing on him, doing his homework, bringing him food, damn near selling their souls for him yet he wanted me. He constantly chased me and made advances towards me. He was not my type of guy in any way, shape or form but eventually, I gave in, and we started dating even though I knew I had Ben, it didn't matter because they would never find out about each other.

Thomas wasn't from a rich family matter of fact his family was below average, but I didn't care because he excited me, he brought out the freak in me. I went from the shy, reserved introverted popular girl to sitting on my desk in class making out with my boyfriend not caring who walked in on us. I was a girl in love or shall I say lust! While my heart fully belonged to Thomas at the time, I had become Ben's full-time sugar baby, I was seeing him two to three times a week after school and even though we weren't having sex he was still so delighted to be in my presence, and he spoiled me silly. I went from three hundred dollars and naira notes to thousands of dollars and expensive gifts he got me every time he travelled.

You're probably wondering what happened to Italy? Well, I found out Ben was trafficking young girls to Italy to become prostitutes and sell drugs for him, crazy! right? Any hoo, I was cashing out with this man and all I had to do was look cute, spend time with him and stroke his ego a little and I would walk out of there a couple of hundred dollar bills richer. The fear of my mother stumbling on all this money I had stashed in my closet worried me and I had to make a move so guess what I started doing? One day I went to school and in the middle of Thomas 'and I's make-out session I stuffed a couple of hundred-dollar bills in his pocket secretly and when he realized what I had done by the end of the school day, he was astounded. The questions started coming in, questions I couldn't answer so I would lie through my teeth and some part of me felt like he knew I was lying but there was nothing he could do but accept it because, in all honesty, he needed it more than I did. I continued spoiling him with the money I was gifted and sometimes Ben would buy me phones and I would give them to Thomas because again I was getting these things at home from my parents.

On this dreadful day, I don't know what Ben drank or smoked but he called me and demanded I come to see him immediately. He was lodged at a guest house 10 minutes away from my house. I made up excuses as to why I couldn't. It was already past 6 pm and my mother who owned a clothing boutique on the same street as this guesthouse got home at 7 pm every day. There was no way I would make it to him and back without getting caught outside by my mom. I tried to wiggle out of this meetup, but he demanded and stood his ground. But why must it be now I asked, and he boldly and bluntly said because I want to taste you and I want to taste you now! I laughed and said, "you can't be serious, right?" but to my demise, he was dead serious. We argued about my virginity, but it fell on deaf ears. I had already stood my ground- no sex, so it was not happening, but something happened, and it opened a new doorway to escape.

Ben said to me "if you come right now and give me what I want, I will give you one thousand dollars cash and two hundred thousand naira extra". Woah! Now that was another level unlocked huh? One thousand what? Two hundred what? No way in hell was I losing out on that deal but there was also no freaking way I was going to give up my virginity to this moron. So, I came up with a plan!

Chapter 4

Big Time Pimping

As I sat there thinking of a master plan, absolutely nothing came to mind. I had no plan, but I was determined to walk away with that money one way or the other. Then boom the thought came into my head. *Use Ogechi*. Ogechi was my maid at the time, she oversaw everything that had to do with my brother and me and the entire house, she cooked, cleaned and assisted my mom with everything else.

We grew up with both a female maid and a male maid commonly known as a house girl and house boy. The male maid lived in the boy's quarter (a little house in the back of the main house) while Ogechi had a room in the main house with us. She was a very pretty girl with a phenomenal physique, and she could pass as an older friend or sister of mine. She was like a family to us and my brother and I loved her dearly compared to all the others we had in the past.

I ran to her immediately and bluntly said *would you like to make two hundred dollars and fifty thousand naira?* Her face lit up with excitement as she said *yes how?*. So I broke the plan down to her. She was to follow me to Ben's guesthouse and give him the best sex of his life and she had to try her best to stay mute. I didn't want her to say anything because her English wasn't as polished as mine. I had 10 mins to get her ready and leave the house, so I began. I took one of my mother's wigs and put it on her, did her makeup and threw on one of the shortest skirts I owned on her with one of my cute crop tops. House girl where? Ogechi had been reborn she was badass and I realized at that moment I had met my very own sex replacement. As we left the house and hurried down to the main gate, the stares of people on our street made me uncomfortable because they all knew she was my maid and wondered why she was dressed like a hooker? Who cares what they thought, we hopped on a bike - okada as Nigerians call it and headed to his guesthouse. As he opened the door and saw us both he had a look of confusion and said what's going on and I responded by telling him since I couldn't give him what he wanted I brought him someone who could. He disagreed at first, but Ogechi took things up a notch and took off her top. She needed the money badly and saw this as a lifetime opportunity. As he saw her breast dangle in front of him, he immediately began removing his clothes, the deal had been sealed. As Ogechi took off her clothes, I demanded the entire money upfront before anything would happen. He hesitated and instead of giving me, he promised he would give it after, but I refused because I didn't trust him one bit. He was already aroused and could barely think straight so I used this to my advantage. I pestered him some more and he had no choice but to hand me the money. He handed me every single bill that was promised, and I thanked him for a job well done. As I turned to walk out of the room and give them privacy to enjoy themselves, he stopped me and insisted I sit on the bed beside them and watch. *No freaking way! That was not in my plan, how was I going to escape this*, I tried to talk my way out of it but he was not bulging one bit so I gave in to his request. I sat there and watched this man aggressively ravish my maid. The entire time I was thinking to myself *"is this what he thought he was going to do to me ha-ha yeah right he must be insane"*

Ogechi put her all into satisfying Ben, I watched her sweat profusely as she did everything. This man had her doing all kinds of tricks and splits- eww it made me sick to my stomach. I was so uncomfortable and so was Ogechi, but she handled it like a champ. This rendezvous went on for about forty minutes until he was satisfied, and she was defeated. When he finally allowed us to go, the speed at which we ran out of there was unbelievable. We jumped on the first bike we saw and told him to take us home at full speed. While on our way, I was apologizing profusely to Ogechi and making sure she was not angry with me in any way. I felt so bad for what she went through and felt the need to make it right.

As is the usual Lagos life, we met traffic on our way home and were stuck in it for a while. While stuck in a little traffic jam we turned to our left and two cars away from us was my mom's car. We were so shocked; we literally almost fell off that bike in a panic attack. *"Hey,*

*Mr. man can you hurry up and get us out of her*e? " Ogechi screamed at the okada man as he drew back and squeezed into the tiny space on the right and continued the journey. He got us home fast enough and luckily, my mother didn't catch us.

As we got home, I gave her what she earned and even threw in something extra on the side and hugged her and apologized once more. As I continued to apologise, I noticed she was more excited about the money she made than my apology, and to my surprise, she said to me *"please, if he wants again, I don't mind"* I was shocked. You mean after what I just witnessed you go through; you still don't mind doing it again. Well, whatever floats her boat, I guess. The things money will make you do!

That day became the first of my many days of pimping girls to Ben. Over the next few weeks, Ben continuously asked to be hooked up with Ogechi, I guess he enjoyed her body, and I enjoyed the money I was getting so did she. Everyone was satisfied, but was Ben truly satisfied? No. He claimed that he imagined me every time he had sex with her and slowly his demands for me increased. It went from me just sitting on the bed to him asking me to stroke his arm while he was with ogechi. Then he would ask for me to strip so I began by removing one piece of clothing like my top and every time he demanded something new, the price went up, I would ask for an increase, and he had no choice but to oblige.

Over the next couple of weeks of consistently sleeping with Ogechi, he grew tired of her and decided to stop. Ogechi was heartbroken. All along, I didn't realize that Ogechi had started falling in love with this man or was it the money she fell in love with? Now that Ogechi was out of the picture I needed to come up with a new plan because Ben had started pestering me for sex again. In the meantime, I avoided his calls for a couple of weeks while I gathered a new strategy.

Back in school, the love between Thomas and I had grown stronger, and he had officially become my personal bank account. I hid all my sugar baby earnings with him and eventually came clean to him about how I made all that money. I had completely changed Thomas' life around. I gave him bragging rights, I gave him confidence so much that he became arrogant! The whispers of how I was spoiling Thomas had spread throughout the hallways and now all the boys wanted a piece of the action and all the girls wanted to know how I was getting all that money, they all wanted in. As time went on, more and more girls had come to me to "put them on" whatever I was doing to make all this money and I opened up to the few I trusted. I told them about Ben. Over the next couple of months, I pimped almost all the girls in my class to Ben. One at a time they approached me during school hours to hook them up with the man that was spending all this money on me and by evening I would get them an appointment to sleep with Ben for five hundred dollars while I would pocket another five hundred without me even having to show up. The business was booming. I was making a fortune off other girls' sexual innuendos all while keeping my virginity, how insane was that?

Unfortunately, Ben would only have sexual intercourse with the girls I sent him not more than twice, so I was running out of girls fast. I needed to act quickly. As time went on rumours spread to other girls in different schools and they all wanted in, my phone was ringing off the hook. I had different girls calling me daily, so much there was a long line. Some who knew me showed up to my house to plead with me to bump them up in line, before I knew what was going on I had girls offering to pay me money to get hooked up with Ben. It was a mess. At this point, I had realized that I had gone way too far, and I was hanging off the deep end. I had started fully pimping secondary school girls.

The pressure had become so much on me, girls had become desperate, and I just couldn't shake the feeling that if I didn't stop, I would get into some big trouble. So, I quit cold turkey, stopped picking up his calls and stopped sending girls his way. I was done! Enough was enough! Slowly I didn't realize Ben had turned me into a trafficker providing him with underage girls.

A month after I had ditched Ben, Maria came home from school and out of excitement, I rushed down to her house to welcome her home. Upon arrival, I noticed her reception towards me had changed. She was cold and distant. I thought it was only due to a bad day so I would let her rest and return the next day. The next day was worse. The reception I got was even worse than the previous day so at this point, I decided to be the bigger person and ask what the attitude was about. She turned to me and asked, *"are you sleeping with Ben?"* I responded with an *"eww no,"* because that was the truth. If she had asked if I were dating Ben then the answer would have been different, but that's not what she asked, was it? *Why would you think that?* I asked, and she said a little birdie had told her of my escapades with him. I stood there in a confused state, not knowing the outcome of this conversation then Maria said to me *"well since you can't be honest with me then we don't need to be friends"* and asked me to leave her house. I was so offended and walked out without even attempting to redeem myself. Ben had cost me my dignity, my sanity and now my friendship with Maria.

On the other hand, I had fallen head over heels for Thomas and to my best knowledge, he felt the same about me. Our relationship was going great, we had everything we wanted and needed courtesy of my previous dealings with Ben - life was great. Although I had told Thomas about my virginity and we weren't having sex, he didn't fully believe me. I couldn't blame him though. He saw my dealings with the girls and knew about all the money so it was hard for him to believe I was not giving my body in exchange for all of it.

On this fateful day, I invited Thomas to my house for the first time since we had started dating and he was delighted to honour my invitation. I knew my parents weren't going to be around, so we had the entire house to ourselves. I had an entire lineup of how I would keep him entertained. I had Ogechi cook something nice and I bought some horror movies that we would watch.

By the time he came over I had the living room set up in a very romantic way. It was dark, cold with candles lit up everywhere. He walked in and was impressed with the effort I had put in, I couldn't have been more excited. As I played the first movie, we barely got a moment to watch it because Thomas couldn't keep his hands off me. He fiddled and fondled with me the entire movie until I gave in and we started kissing. Halfway into our make out session things had taken a drastic turn and before I knew what was going on Thomas was on top of me with his pants down. The fear of losing my virginity in that moment plagued me. I still didn't feel ready I was scared, scared of the commitment that came with sex.

Growing up as a female in a Nigerian home all you are ever taught is that if you have sex with a boy pregnancy will ensue. I knew I wasn't ready to get pregnant, so I withdrew but Thomas had reached a point of no return, he was going to have sex with me whether I was ready or not. As I began to try to wiggle myself from under him telling him to stop whatever he was doing as I had changed my mind, it fell on deaf ears. Rather than let me go, he tightened his grip while forcefully kissing me to shut me up, before I knew what was going on he had forcefully stuck his two fingers inside of me. As I felt his fingers, I screamed out loud because the pain I had just felt was indescribable. I pleaded for him to stop but my discomfort seemed to encourage him to keep going. I began begging him to stop but instead he continued to force his way and forcefully penetrated me, completely ignoring my pain. Just like that at 17 I lost my virginity on our living room floor most horribly and painfully ever.

As he finished and stood up, he made his way over to switch the lights on. That was when he discovered the bloodstains all over him and realized truly, I was a virgin. It became awkward and uncomfortable for him and immediately he realized his mistake, He knelt in front of me and started pleading for forgiveness. Well, the deed had been done, I couldn't go back in time to erase what had just happened, but I couldn't deny I still loved him even though he just hurt me. So, I forgave him and continued like nothing happened.

Over the next few days, he continued begging and asking for forgiveness, but the truth is I had already forgiven him, and it didn't change the way I felt about him. Rather I became solely dependent on his affection, I had become vulnerable and well since I wasn't a virgin anymore, I'm sure you know how this story went. We were having a lot of sex and I mean a lot, you name it, in the bathroom at school, his friend's house, my house and at parties, anywhere we had a room and some privacy. Thomas exposed me to a new level of bad behaviour but in his arms, I found solace, I felt safe.

Chapter 5

The Major Heartbreak

It was summer and as our usual custom, we were to travel to the US for a family vacation. This vacation was for Brian and I mainly because my mother had her medical checkup and decided to take us along.

We had arrived in Maryland Baltimore as we would be spending the next couple of weeks with cousins while mommy attended her medical visits. She had been battling cancer for the last 6 months and her doctor had informed her of the possibilities of her cancer spreading. Due to our age our mother shielded us from the truth regarding her illness and for all we knew we had come to America for a vacation, the three of us like old times.

We spent most of our days shopping and eating at restaurants while other days we sat in the house while she attended her doctor's appointments. We were oblivious of what was going on, our relatives did a good job of keeping us in the dark. On this fateful day we woke up excited to get ready for the day's adventure when mommy's phone rang. It was the phone call that would change our lives forever. As we were getting dressed we heard a loud scream from the kitchen.

I was scared to the bones and was wondering what could have happened. *Who called her? What happened?* All these questions plagued my mind as I ran downstairs to see what all the ruckus was about. As we approached the kitchen, we saw our mother on the floor crying her eyes out while my aunt consoled her telling her everything is going to be okay. *What is going to be okay?* I wondered.

As soon as we walked in, I could see my mother struggling to pick herself up, but the tears held her down. My aunt immediately rushed to her defense and hurried us out of the kitchen. While we sat down in the living room waiting for mommy to come out with a smile on her face and tell us to continue getting dressed, she never did.

The doctor said my cancer has spread significantly and I might need more management than before. I will be sending you to New York to stay with your cousins while I stay here and begin my chemotherapy treatment. This was what she said to my brother and I when she eventually came out of the kitchen. As the words came out, all I could think of was how could she abandon us like that, and ship us off to other people? The selfish brat in me ignored the part about treatment and cancer and focused only on the vacation I thought she just ruined.

My mom was going through the hardest time in her life and all I could think about was returning to Nigeria to continue my relationship with Thomas not because I didn't care but because I didn't understand, and maybe I didn't care too. We continued the rest of our trip by ourselves talking to our mom twice a day and eventually returned to Nigeria without her.

As much as I missed my mom, I was ecstatic to be reunited with my boyfriend and we continued right where we left off sex, sex, and more sex. Something was different, I seemed to have had more freedom than usual. I was staying out later than usual, sneaking Thomas in more often and partying almost every day. My dad was so occupied and spent more time away from home and I was loving the freedom. My brother had resumed boarding school so part of me loved the new living arrangements. I was alone at home and had freedom like no other. I missed my mother and brother sometimes and wished they were home with me but that feeling barely lasts for hours because Thomas is either close by or there is another party I can attend. The odds were in my favor, and I had finally started living the life I wanted with no one to answer too. All the adults in my life seemed too busy to care about what I had going on and I didn't mind.

Days turned into weeks, and I hadn't heard my mother's voice which was quite unusual because she always kept to her schedule. She always made sure to call me every day at 6pm not only to talk to me but to speak to Linda who was our maid at the time. Linda was the new maid we hired after my mother fired Ogechi. Apparently, she had been sleeping with every dick and harry on our street which eventually got her pregnant. My neighbor who was friends with my mom broke the news to her about Ogechi's street man-hoping antics, and she was instantly fired. I couldn't help but blame myself, I had introduced her to a means of making fast cash and she ran with it. Linda had barely spent three months with us, and I didn't really care for her, so she stayed out of my cross hairs. Whenever mommy called, I had to be home because she would insist on speaking to Linda. Not like she couldn't call Linda directly, but I assumed it was her way of keeping tabs on me.

I was getting worried, why hadn't she called? What was keeping her so occupied? I began asking questions, but I was not getting answers. This particular night, I felt a high level of unease. I tossed and turned all night, something was heavy on my heart, and I didn't even know what it was. I couldn't sleep, I was anxious for no reason, I felt so uneasy. My father returned that night reeking of alcohol, came into my room, sat on the bed beside me and as I turned to look at him, he said *"when you wake up in the morning, pack your things I'm taking you to your aunt's house"*

Is it the alcohol talking, or does he mean what he just said? What is happening in my aunt's house and why do I have to be there? And why did he have to tell me this late? I shrugged it off and concluded it must be the alcohol intake, and eventually fell asleep.

Although I couldn't place it, something felt quite different that night. By morning time my father had come into my room again to remind me someone will pick me up and take me to my aunt's (moms' younger sisters) house shortly, so I needed to get ready. *What's the rush? I just woke up and have not had the time to prepare na?* I said. He ignored me and walked out of my room. I grudgingly put a few things in my weekend bag and got ready. As I went downstairs to have breakfast, my aunt's maid (Ada) greeted me with a hug. She noticed I was about to have my breakfast, so she waited for me. Everything was moving so fast, and I could barely keep up. I felt overwhelmed.

As I sat there eating breakfast, I noticed a group of people in the living room with my dad and it seemed like a gathering of sad faces. *What could have happened? Why are they looking sad?* As I walked in to acknowledge the faces, he sent me out and slammed the door. *What the hell?* I was over it at this point. How rude! I turned to Ada and said, "*let's go*" and we walked out of the house without even saying goodbye. As I arrived at my aunt's house, I met my cousins at home. My aunt had three- all male. They had been at home all day waiting for me. Unfortunately, I wasn't too thrilled to see them because I felt everybody spoiled my plans. I was supposed to spend the weekend with Thomas but here I was all the way across town stuck with these three knuckleheads. I stormed into the house and walked straight upstairs to the guest bedroom, flipped the ac switch on and went back to sleep.

A couple hours later my phone rang, and I jumped out of bed. Thomas had been calling me and I had to break the unfortunate news of me canceling our weekend plans to him.

Babe are you serious? I was really looking forward to spending this weekend with you? I even got you something, He said.

Really? What is it?,

I'm not telling you till I see you

That's not fair you know

What's not fair is me not seeing you this weekend, He replied

Don't worry I will get out of here as soon as I can and be in your arms again. I miss you so much

I miss you too baby

As I ended the call, I fantasized about how the weekend would have turned out, if my dad hadn't shipped me down here and I got angry all over again.

As my aunt returned home that evening with her friends she looked as if she had been crying all day, her face was swollen and red while her eyes had sunken and everyone

around her looked equally as sad. I greeted her and continued about my day. Later, that evening, she called me into her room. As I walked in, three of her friends sat on the bed beside her. She asked me to take a seat and I thought *what the hell was going on? Why is everyone acting weird?*

It felt like I was in a twilight zone. My aunt's friend began asking me a bunch of irrelevant questions and I wondered why they were beating around the bush because it was obvious, they were hiding something from me. She handed me a Bible and asked me to open it to a particular verse. I can't remember the exact verse but as I tried to find the verse, I kept wondering what this was all about. When I did, she asked me to read the verse out loud. At this point, I had become uncomfortable, but I did as she asked. As I concluded the verse, she said to me "I *asked you to read this verse because I want you to know that God is with you*" I replied with a long *okaaaaaaay* as I sat there in a confused state. I was not ready for the next couple of words that came out of her mouth, and even if I was given a lifetime to prepare, I don't think I'll ever be ready. She said *"your mother is dead"*

I felt a wave of rage trim down my spine. The only words I could mutter was *"is this a joke?"*. I scanned the faces in the room hoping for someone to laugh out loud and say "Got ya!". Seconds turned to Minutes, and nobody laughed. *"They are serious, they are really serious, this is not a joke"* I turned to look at her sister one more time still hoping for her to say something but instead she broke down in tears. That was the confirmation. My mother is actually dead.

I felt everything at once - anger, sadness, rage, betrayal, defeat and guilt. I blanked for a minute trying to figure out these emotions. I have never felt this way before, this is beyond getting your heart broken, this is beyond sadness. This is a whole new level of emotion. I jumped up, flinging the bible in my hand and looking to fling anything else I could. That was when they held me down. In this position, I started to feel everything again- all at once. Then the tears came, it consumed me whole. I felt like I was in a dark hole - a dark hole so thick it consumed me.

I cried for hours, alone in the dark, with a million thoughts running through my mind. Now it all made sense, the weird acts from everyone, why she had not called me for weeks, why everyone was being so nice to me, the restlessness I felt the night before, why my dad came home smelling like he had taken a bath in whiskey; the pieces were all starting to come together.

I was filled with rage! I hated everyone and everything, I hated my dad even more, somehow, I felt it was his fault. If we had never moved down here this wouldn't have happened, maybe if he was more invested in his marriage and not chasing after my school moms, MAYBE JUST MAYBE SHE WOULD STILL BE ALIVE!

Why was everyone else alive and she had to die? It was unfair. Part of me doubted her death and every day I hoped someone would tell me it was a sick joke, that it never happened. Another part of me believed that she would resurrect, or they would find out they rushed the judgement, and she was still alive. I went to bed every night and woke up waiting for the good news, I was in denial.

Depression started to set in. Although I was surrounded by people, I felt alone. It felt like I was the only one in the world. My cousins tried their best to keep me entertained while everyone else tried to keep my mind off it. I would fake a smile so they could leave me alone. Deep down, I just wanted to end it all - the pain, the sadness, the hurt, the grief, everything. I wanted to close my eyes and put an end to everything.

Chapter 6

Coping

I cried myself to sleep every night and woke up with tears in my eyes. Back at home funeral arrangements had started and school had gone on recess, so that meant Brian was coming home. The plan was for him to join me here and to be honest I wasn't looking forward to seeing him. I couldn't stand to face him let alone break this news to him, he was only 13 at the time, how was he going to handle that? I refused to be in the same room as they broke the news to him. I stayed away from him for days. I avoided coming in contact with him. A part of me couldn't handle seeing him heartbroken so I thought the best thing to do was to let him grieve alone the same way I did.

The death of my mother had become an unspoken Truth. As much as we suffered, we chose to each suffer in silence, no one addressing their pain or emotions. The next couple of weeks were long and painful as we watched them plan and execute her burial. I remember glancing at her cold, lifeless body thinking God would feel our pain and hear our cries and wake her up. I watched them lower her into the ground and pour sand on top of her tombstone, she was buried in my father's village in Anambra state and the events of that day sent me down a downward spiral.

I had become a shadow of myself, nothing or no one else mattered. I refused to talk to anyone, even Thomas. I didn't need anyone trying to console me or justify why my mother had to die. I wanted to stay angry, I wanted to feel the rage, I wanted to be depressed, I had a right to be, my best friend was gone, the only parent I had grown to know was gone. *Who was going to take care of me? Of us? Who was going to raise us? How were we going to survive life? Who was going to make sure Brian was okay?*

I know we had another parent, but it really didn't seem like we did.

After the burial, we returned to Lagos and back to our house with our dad. His presence aggravated me. Brian was taken back to school while I remained at home by myself with nothing but my sorrow and pain. I avoided everyone, a part of me felt like an outcast, my mother's death increased my insecurities. Asides from not constantly wanting to repeat the story to people I started to feel like my mother's death was a stain to my reputation. Whatever made me feel like that, I don't know. My mind had taken me to a dark place, and I had started to question life and my purpose on earth. Nothing made sense to me anymore, I had no reason to live.

When Ben heard the news of my mother's death, he reached out to me. I was surprised to see his call and was excited at the same time. I was still not in the mood to speak with anyone, but I picked his call. From one condolence to talking everyday. Although I had cut him off earlier, he was the only person I felt comfortable with. Slowly we began our secret relationship again. I was a broken mess and needed company. Ben was happy that I had returned to him and agreed to take things slow. He gave me space to heal and never pestered me for sex even though he could sense my vulnerability. I was at my lowest and to be honest if he pushed a little harder, he just might have been lucky.

I visited him every day and he made sure to cheer me up in his little way. I started drinking a lot more courtesy of Ben and he would always try to get me to smoke cigarettes and weed with him. I was familiar with cigarettes because my father smoked them all day and I puffed on a few of his sticks in the past for fun but weed was unfamiliar territory. Ben would constantly try to shove his weed down my throat, but I would constantly refuse, I was too scared. I watched him snort a couple lines of cocaine here and there and every time he would offer, I would instantly shut down his request. Although I was sad, I wasn't ready for drugs. I would smoke a couple cigarettes here and there, so he wouldn't have to offer me the others.

Ben had made so many promises to me at this point that even though I was in no way sexually attracted to him, I had grown a soft spot for him. He offered to take me along with him to Italy and he wanted me to head his operation because he liked the way I had carried myself when hooking him up with all those girls in the past. A part of me still didn't trust Ben, but I figured being with him was better than living in the same house with my dad. So, I agreed to follow him to Italy.

But there was a problem. My dad had my passport and all my other documents, and I knew getting it back would damn near be impossible. I never told Ben this part of it because I was sure I could handle it when the time came. I had become his little madam, we went everywhere together, and I sat in on his drug deals. Yup, I would sit there and watch him distribute his products, his cocaine and we would walk out with bags of cash.

I remember him introducing me to the next batch of girls being shipped off to Italy, most of them were my age or slightly older and he had them sleeping in the boy's quarter of his friend's house. It was a dingy room with one queen sized bed and 6 girls sleeping in it. All I could think of while they walked up to us to greet us was *"so these ones chose to become prostitutes in Italy? How unfair must life have been to them?*

There was this one girl that caught my attention, Yemisi. She was drop dead gorgeous but was unkempt. She could pass as a model, slender, very tall with fair skin. She seemed shy and very unhappy. I decided to stay back to familiarize myself with the girls while Ben went into the main house. As I conversed with them their stories broke my heart. Most of them had either been raped or abused one way or the other and had nothing to live for. I felt a connection to them because I could relate to what they were talking about. I instantly grew a soft spot for them. A part of me wanted to beg them to rethink what they were going to do in Italy but at the same time I couldn't ruin Ben's business.

Yemisi eventually confided in me and informed me of how she was there against her will. She insisted that her father had sold her off to Ben because he had some debts to pay and Yemisi's body was his only bargaining power. She begged me to help her in whatever way I could, and I assured her I would. Being the young naive girl I was, I thought it would be as easy as just asking Ben to let her go, so I did. I even went as far as promising Ben sex in exchange for Yemisi's freedom. He excitedly agreed and told me she would be freed. A couple days later we went back to his friend's house, and I walked to the back to check on the girls. To my surprise Yemisi was still there, she looked like she had just been badly beaten. I walked over to her to find out what happened, but she began shouting at me to leave her alone. She said I caused her a great deal of pain and she had been warned to keep her mouth shut and stay away from me. I stood up and walked out of that room heartbroken. I truly thought I had helped her, but I only made things worse for her and now she had been beaten badly.

As I walked back to the main house the realization of who Ben was and what he did feared me, I was way in over my head and playing a dangerous game. Ben was a criminal, and a lowlife and if I wasn't careful, I would end up hurt. I began to avoid Ben and consequently cut all ties with him.

Two weeks later as I returned home my dad and a female family friend were waiting for me in the living room. I was scared and wondering what this meeting was all about. From the look on their faces, it didn't seem like it was something good.

Did something bad happen? Hopefully not. I thought

As I approached them and greeted them, the next thing I heard was "*Who is Ben?*"

For some reason, I felt relieved. At least something bad has not happened. As I processed the best lie to tell them. The woman started telling me of the many people that told her about my involvement with Ben. How they always saw me in front of his car.

Wow! I thought

I don't know anybody called Ben o, I denied

Come on, shut up there. I saw you and him leaving a guest house weeks ago

Aunty it is not me you saw, I continued to deny

The argument went on for hours, but I insisted I didn't know any Ben. At some point, my dad got so angry and flared up. He scolded me so bad while my Aunty started lecturing me on why I should stay away from someone like Ben. They kept going back and forth but to be honest I was not listening. I had zoned out and all their advice just sounded like noise to me.

Exhausted and frustrated, my dad said "*You are going back to America. I cannot control you anymore.*"

What? This man can't be serious I thought

Apparently, he was more serious than I thought

Chapter 7

Coming To America

Few days to my departure from Nigeria. I reached out to Ben and told him about what had transpired between my dad and me. He told me of his involvement with her. Apparently, they dated a few years back and she had found it hard to move on. He claimed she became jealous and possessive of him which explained her coming to report me. I wasn't surprised, it will be hard to leave someone like Ben, considering how generous he is. He apologized for all the trouble he put me in and insisted on flying me to Italy immediately. As a smart girl, I played along with his plan and requested some money from him to prepare myself for the trip to Italy. He gave me $4,000 and 1 million naira and told me to get everything I wanted and prepare to leave for Italy at the end of the month. Upon collecting the money, I got home, blocked his numbers, packed my bags and headed back to my aunt's house where I hid until I left for the states.

A week later, I was back in Houston, and I was truly happy for the first time in a while. This was home, I was back where I truly belonged. I felt relieved to be away from Ben and the traumas surrounding me in Nigeria. I began living with an aunt of mine. I was enrolled in college and began working. Life was slowly returning to normal, but this was a new normal- something I was not used to.

I would get up daily, dress for school and head to work after school. I worked for another aunt who owned a home health facility where I cared for mentally challenged adults. The job seemed scary at first and I thought how in the hell was this suitable for me. I continued living this average life and was grateful for it. After everything I had experienced in Nigeria this was the change I needed, but deep down I wondered how long it would last.

Even though I had started life all over and I seemed happier, depression still loomed in my heart. I still sulked over my mother's death, and I questioned my existence more often. The fact that I had been separated from everything and everyone I was used to made me even sadder. I couldn't cope with this new routine and before I knew it the depression had taken over again. The pressure had become too much for me. I couldn't sleep at night, I had no one to talk to because I hated everyone. I wasn't doing very well in school; I began skipping out on classes and eventually dropped out. Every school day, I would dress up for school and get dropped off at school, but I never entered the building.

At the end of the semester when my grades were released, I was not surprised at all. I had failed every single course I enrolled into. My aunt was furious, and I could understand her frustration. She spent a lot of time and money. I couldn't care less, however, I didn't even want to be in school, I didn't want to work, I just wanted to be left alone. Nobody understood what I was going through because they would not just leave me alone.

My aunt and I began arguing a lot. She insisted, she would not tolerate my behavior while I lived under her roof. So, guess what I did? I moved out. I had just turned 18 and I knew I was of legal age to live on my own. Since I had a job and my own car, I thought I could take care of myself and besides I needed my freedom. I was tired of living by my aunts' rules. I had been living on my own terms for the past year and now she expects me to abide by her strict rules. I just couldn't deal.

At work, I had become friends with a Nigerian girl who had the same name as me. She loved everything about me and was really nice to me. She was a couple years older than I was and had been living with her mom who also worked with us. I persuaded her to move in with me so we could split the bills. She was excited at the offer, and in no time, we had moved into our first apartment. The moving process was a breeze. I barely had anything to move except my clothes. I came back from work one night, stood in front of my aunt and broke the news to her.

"I'm moving out, I already have a place and I'll be moving in tomorrow!" she sat there in disbelief wondering how I was able to pull that off right under her nose. When she recovered from the initial shock of the news, she tried talking me out of it.

You are still young and cannot handle the challenges of living alone. Think about the bills you will have to pay. I know living alone sounds rosy, but it is not as rosy as it seems. Please think through this properly. She said in a surprisingly calm manner. Deep down I knew she was right, but I just didn't care. All I wanted was my freedom and I was determined to get it. On the morning of the next day, I said my final goodbyes, packed my luggage and drove off. Off to my new adult life.

Within two weeks, I had settled into my new apartment, changed schools and started taking fashion classes while modeling on the side. I was living my dream life. I would drive from school to photoshoots and back to work almost every other day. The routine had become exhausting, I was stressed, tired and unhappy. I thought i was going to be happier living on my own, but I was wrong. I couldn't continue like this, something had to change. I dropped out of school again but kept my job because I needed the money.

I was working round the clock. I was taking all kinds of modelling gigs- promo photoshoots, paid shoots I took them all, modeling became my life. One day, while packing up to head to work after an intense photo shoot session I met a fellow model Amber, a 6-foot-tall dark-skinned goddess. I had never seen such a beautiful dark-skinned girl like her. She had been in the industry for 5 years and was very experienced. She knew the ins and out, and the dos and don'ts of the industry. She was sweet enough to give me some pointers to make my modelling journey easier. I thanked her and asked her to become my mentor in which she obliged.

Over the next few months, we became friends. Amber was 21 which meant she was old enough to drink alcohol and she drank a lot of it, safe to say she was an alcoholic. On the other hand, I was only 18 and could not consume alcohol. However, Amber didn't care, she always said if I didn't get caught in public drinking alcohol, I was good. Amber partied a lot, she was living the model life I had only seen on TV, and I wanted in, but my age kept me back. It made me furious that I couldn't attend the same industry parties she always attended. Unlike Amber, who lived in a penthouse with her 46-year-old Caucasian sugar daddy, I had to work to pay all my bill. I sometimes wondered what life would be like If I was in Amber's shoes.

On this faithful Saturday morning, my phone rang. It was a call from Amber. I was surprised to see a call from her at that time.

Hey Amber, What's up? I asked curiously

Pack a weekend bag up, we are going to Miami, she replied hurriedly

Miami? Really? How?

I was invited to a party over there and I managed to get you a pass so stop asking so many questions and pack a weekend bag

I was super excited. Finally, I am going to attend a party with the big shots present. Can you imagine that? I was already lost in my imaginations thinking of the different kinds of people I could meet. *Would I meet my own sugar daddy who will finally take care of my bills and put me in his luxury penthouse? What will this party be like?* A lot of questions flooded my mind as I headed to her house. At that moment, I forgot I was underaged all that mattered was *I was going to Miami baby!*

As I approached the front of her building, I saw her waiting for me downstairs. As I pulled up and got out of the car, I handed the valet my keys and hopped in her beautiful Porsche and we sped off to the airport. The entire time I wondered what she had up her sleeve. *What's the plan?* I asked out of excitement, and she replied, *"wait and see, you're going to have the best time of your life"*. I sat back and enjoyed the ride, Miami here we come!

We boarded our flight, found our seats and before I knew it Amber had started requesting for drinks. One thing led to another, and we both walked off that plane drunk and ready to party. As we arrived in Miami, we hurried down to the hotel and got ready to hit the streets the Miami style. At 10 pm we called a taxi and headed down to the party. *"Amber, how will I get in? I'm only 18, remember?"* I asked. She giggled and responded with *"this is an industry party, no one cares about your age"* I felt confident. She clearly had a plan to get me in, well I hoped she did.

We pulled up to a big white mansion in the middle of nowhere. From the outside it looked like a museum that had been closed, but upon driving in we could hear the music blasting. My heart began beating faster and faster and my palms were sweaty. I was so nervous. As we pulled up to the main gates, we were approached by two hefty security guards. They looked so scary as they requested a code which Amber provided. And just like that we were let into the premises.

Here I was at my first industry event, it felt surreal. All my fashion shows and photoshoots had finally paid off. I couldn't contain my excitement. As we walked into the front door Amber turned to me and said, *"you should probably keep your age to yourself tonight, you wouldn't want anyone treating you like a child"*. Truly that was the last thing I wanted, I was grown, and I want to be treated accordingly.

As we walked in, my mind was completely blown away. It was more than I ever imagined. It was so beautiful, electric, and loud. Everyone was drunk and seemed to be having the time of their lives. Everywhere I turned alcohol was being served, I had never seen anything like it. Amber pulled me and we went straight to the bar, grabbed our champagne flutes, took two shots of patrons to the head and made our way to the dance floor. It was my first-time taking shots and although I didn't know what I was drinking I didn't care. If everyone at this party was drinking it then who was I not to want it.

We danced and danced while sipping on our champagne and occasionally she would request for more shots. We had so many drinks that I lost count. An hour into the party the DJ stopped the music and announced the arrival of two of the top platinum A list r & b artists at the time and I almost shit my pants. *Oh my God!* little ole Amanda was in the same building with her celebrity crush. He was right across from me; I was looking at him and he was looking in my direction. It felt too good to be true. I waited for the dream to be over, so I would wake up, but I was still there right across from this man, this fine piece of man. I whispered to Amber how I couldn't believe who I was looking at, she laughed and said *"you're such a newbie"* tapped me on my shoulder and told me to follow her to the bathroom. When we got in the bathroom I couldn't stop going on and on about how I had the biggest crush on this artist and how I wanted to marry him. She laughed and begged me not to embarrass her out there, I promised her I wouldn't, even though I wasn't sure how I would behave myself with all the numerous I had taken.

The alcohol started kicking in and my head started spinning. I needed to sit down for a minute, I needed water, I felt uneasy, the room started spinning and Amber could tell. "*Hey, hey, hey just relax, you will be just fine*". She pulled out a little glass jar from her purse and emptied the contents on the sink counter, pulled out her credit card and a hundred-dollar bill and told me to snort a line and smoke a cigarette. Here I was faced with another decision to do cocaine, I refused. She laughed and pushed me out the way, bent over and snorted everything she had poured on the counter while I stood there like a lost puppy. As she got back up, she said *"I remember when I turned down my first line too, the boring old days"*. She cleaned her face, wiped off the counter and placed a purple pill in my palm. I asked what it was and what I was supposed to do with it, she told me it was ecstasy, and I was supposed to place it under my tongue. *It would make you feel relaxed*, she said. *It was just a little pill, what was the worst it could do to me?* I thought as I put it in my mouth.

I had never heard of ecstasy until that very moment, and no one had ever given me a pep talk as to what it would do to me that day. We walked out of the bathroom and went back to the dancefloor to continue our rave and at this point I could no longer keep up. It felt like my head was no longer on my body, the room started changing colors and I could no longer tell my right from my left. I don't know what was in that pill, but it made everything worse, and I started panicking. Amber grabbed my arms and told me to take control of what I was feeling, channel the good vibes and just let the music take control as we danced even more.

We were probably the highest in the room and I don't know what it was we were doing but it got us noticed, everyone wanted in on our fun and in no time, we were invited to the artist table. Slowly my wildest dreams were unraveling before my eyes, but I was too high to even notice. Amber, on the other hand, was having the time of her life. We were asked to follow them and their entourage back to their hotel and of course we agreed. As we made it up to the penthouse suite of The Ritz Carlton, I was ready to go home. I was fagged out, I knew I couldn't hang anymore and as excited I was to be in the presence of my biggest Hollywood crush, I couldn't take it anymore, I feared I was dying. My heart had been beating faster than it should have and my palms were sweaty, so sweaty, I knew I felt weird.

The party continued upstairs but I sat down in a corner of the room to keep my head from spinning so fast. One thing led to another, and I passed out. When I woke up 8 hours later, I was back in my hotel room and Amber was nowhere to be found. I panicked as I tried recollecting my memories from the night before but to no avail, I reached for my phone beside me and tried to call Amber. It rang a couple times and she would send me straight to voicemail. My agitation grew, "*Oh my God I hope Amber is alive, what the hell had happened to us the night before?*" Few minutes later, I got a text message that read; "*hey thanks for embarrassing me last night, I hope you are happy, I thought you were grown but you're still a child and we can't hang, have a safe trip back to Houston!*" I tried calling her one more time, but I was blocked. Just like that my friendship with Amber had ended.

I flew back to Houston alone, got home and told my roommate about how crazy my weekend had been. With everything that had happened in Miami, I had a rethink about modeling. Maybe I wasn't cut out for that life just yet, I was wild but not wild enough for this, so I decided to give modeling a break and focus on working.

Chapter 8

Texas

I had started dating Dami, a Nigerian. I met him at a friend's birthday party in Houston. I felt a connection to him from the first day we met. He was sweet, and a real gentleman. Since Thomas, I hadn't been in any other relationship and Dami would be the first. He was slightly older than me; I was 19 and he was 22. He was more established and already had his life planned out. We had the best moments together; our connection was great. I spent most of my free time with him and he did with me too. We did everything together; we had become inseparable and over time our families had become familiar.

I spent so much time with him that I didn't see the point of paying my lease the next month because I was barely at my house anyway. So, I waited until my lease expired and instantly moved in with him. My roommate was against it and she tried to talk me out of it but I was in love and nothing or anyone could convince me not to move in with Dami at the time. I was sad I had to leave my roommate stranded but the joy of staying with Dami trumped the guilt and sadness I felt for her.

It's been six months of bliss with Dami, our relationship was still waxing so strong it felt like a dream. One morning, I woke up with a horrible taste in my mouth, like I had been chewing on metal the night before. I wondered what could have happened then thought it must have been something I ate the day before. All through that day, I felt fatigued, I barely had the strength to do anything. My body felt more like I had been overworked. I told my supervisor how I felt, and he let me leave work early that day. On getting home, I took a hot shower and went back to sleep. Dami returned home much later in the evening and met me still asleep. He was surprised because he knew I wouldn't normally be asleep at that time. He woke me up and asked what was wrong.

My whole body feels so sore, and I feel very tired and stressed out. I replied. *So sorry babe, you should stay home and relax till you feel better.* He said as he planted a kiss on my forehead.

The next morning came and I didn't feel any better and my condition started to get worse as the days went by. I immediately knew something was off because I hardly fall sick, and this was becoming more than just tired. I started to research these symptoms on google and all I could see was the word pregnant.

Me, pregnant? What would 19-year-old me possibly do with a child?

I was still a child, I was still figuring life out and although I had been dating a man who had his shit together, I was in no way ready for the commitment a child would bring. I could not bring myself to tell him the news, I was hoping I would wake up and not be pregnant anymore. I don't know why I thought it worked like that. I wished and wished for it to be gone but rather my symptoms grew worse. I was now spending most of my days in bed and the other days in the bathroom where I would be puking my brains out. Even on the days I managed to go to work I would end up clocking out early and heading right to bed. I couldn't keep any food down and I couldn't keep my eyes open to save my life, the energy I was using to vomit had physically and emotionally drained me. Dami didn't notice all of this because he was busy at work and was barely around but whenever he got back and asked about my health, I'll make up an excuse. I wasn't ready to tell him just yet.

Weeks went by, and I was running out of excuses. Dami was already suspicious and he could tell I was not telling him the truth. One day, he demanded to know the truth as to what was going on, I tried to wiggle my way out of telling him, but he will not take no for an answer. Frustrated and Angry, I yelled *I'm pregnant*

He froze!

I could sense he was disappointed from the way he looked at me in the first few seconds, but his next reaction was what confused me. He was excited and for some reason that annoyed me. *How on earth will he be excited at the fact that I am pregnant? Does he not understand the consequence of this? I had made the one mistake my mother constantly warned me about and here he was being all excited.*

So, what are we going to do? I asked, he turned to me and said, "*we are going to have a baby*". *No, we are not,* I said as I stormed out of the kitchen. We spent the next month arguing over me keeping his child. I stood my ground and told him I was too young to have a child. *I will not be a mom at 19 Dami, there is nothing you can say to convince me.* I continued to reiterate, but it felt like the more I said it, the more it drove a wedge between us.

He had threatened to inform my family and his family that I had plans of terminating his child, but I honestly didn't care. Months went by, and my pregnancy bump had grown bigger. All the while, I was looking for an abortion clinic for the procedure but getting one was difficult. When I finally found an abortion clinic, I was told to pay $500 because of how far gone I was, and I only had two and a half weeks before the pregnancy would become permanent. *How was I ever going to raise $500?* I had missed so many days of work there was no way my paycheck would cover it and I knew asking Dami was out of the equation, so I had to come up with a plan fast. I became depressed, not knowing if I would be able to afford to remove this unwanted distraction in my life, but I was determined, nothing was going to get in my way.

On my way to Walmart one afternoon, I was so exhausted from driving all day and running errands. I lost focus and ran a stop sign that was hidden, and boom! I was hit from the back of the passenger side, which sent the car spinning. The car kept spinning till it hit a tree on the right. For a moment, I thought I was dead. Looking around me, I realized I was still alive, and I survived that ghastly accident. While the car was spinning, I hit my head on the window panel. Looking back, it was obvious it was only God that could have spared me from dying because I wasn't even wearing a seatbelt. As I struggled to exit the car, people who had witnessed the crash came to assist me and pulled me out. I had no external injuries but was in a state of shock. All I could think of was how badly my car must have been hit, but to my surprise the damages were minimal.

The woman who hit my car was also pulled out of her car. She ran over to me and began apologizing, her car had been totaled. Although I was at fault and I knew it, I let her believe it was her fault and she offered me cash to fix my car in exchange for not calling the police. I took the cash, drove home and counted my blessings, God had truly come through for me in the weirdest way.

"What happened to your car, who hit you?" Dami asked, *I don't know, it was a hit and run, I didn't get a chance to see who did it,* and just like that the matter died. Two days later I strolled in the clinic and got my abortion done at 13weeks and 3 days. Dami was left in the dark until my friend brought me home that day and walked me upstairs, he took one look at me, shook his head and stormed out of the apartment. At that point, I didn't care, I was in too much pain to consider his feelings.

Recovering from my abortion had to be the worst pain ever. I constantly cried because of the pain I was feeling. I would curl up on the floor wishing for death. I would attempt to overdose sometimes because I just wanted it to end. I couldn't explain the pain to anybody because they wouldn't understand, especially Dami, so I suffered in silence until I had completely healed.

Dami finally forgave me but so much had happened that caused a strain on our relationship. In the 3 years we had been dating, it had become toxic. We were in physical altercations a lot more because I had become so angry and hot tempered and to be honest, I had started losing interest in him. Everything about him had started irritating me and he started reporting me to my dad- which I hated. That was the height of it for me. I needed freedom, I needed space, I needed fresh air so I rebelled.

I began partying a lot and staying out more often. During this period, I met Papa- a fine gentleman and that was how my cheating chronicles began. It was a wild Friday night, my girls and I had ended up in one of Houston's swankiest nightclubs at the time, Belvedere uptown park. Since it was a Friday night, all the hottest Nigerians in the city were out to play, and it was always fun. That would be my first time partying there and I loved it. We walked in and immediately made our way over to the bar, ordered our drinks, and as we grabbed our cocktails, we hit the dance floor. We danced for hours until the waiter walked over to me and tapped me. *"The gentleman over there asked if you and your friends could join their table?"* My friends lit up with excitement as we walked over. As I made my way over to the section, I noticed he had begun creating a space for me besides him and I walked right over to him as he pulled me up on the couch.

He smelt like money and looked like trouble, but I was willing to explore all the possibilities. *"What do you wanna drink?"* he asked *Champagne will do*. He poured me a glass. We partied nonstop and by the end of the night he asked for my phone number and drove off, I never even got his name. Days went by, and I hadn't heard from this mysterious guy. I was upset, like *why didn't I think to ask him for his number instead?* I counted it as a loss and kept it moving. One evening I got a text saying *"hey it's papa from Belv"* he had finally reached out and I couldn't contain my excitement. We chatted all night, the next day and the day after and eventually set up a date for that weekend.

Friday night approached and I sent him my address to pick me up, if you're wondering where Dami was while all of this was happening, he was staying at his father's house. We were getting into so many fights due to him constantly catching me with other guys. Our neighbors were always calling the police on us so he left the house to stay with his dad.

On the night of our first date Papa pulled up to my apartment in a beat-up Toyota. I was confused, *was he pulling my legs, was the real car parked somewhere else? Was this a test to see if I was a gold digger?* I held these thoughts in and jumped into the passenger side. Halfway to our destination the engine shut off and the car stopped in the middle of the street and refused to come on. I was utterly embarrassed but for some reason this guy still seemed so cool, he had a calm to him that was intriguing and that kept me going.

We pulled up to Spindletop, one of the city's most exclusive luxury dining spots built inside a hotel, Hyatt regency and which from the looks of it wasn't cheap. We approached and he requested a valet. This guy was bold, he had guts to think they would park his little beat down Toyota by the fleet of luxury cars that filled the parking lot. As we walked in, I looked back to catch the reaction of the valet guys and they had willingly pulled his car upfront. Wait a minute, something was off, I couldn't read him, this guy was cooler than he let out to be. He grabbed my hand as we walked through the hotel lobby, his grip was firm, yet his hands were so soft and gentle I began imagining what life would be like with him. A guy my age with all this poise and arrogance all in one, I silently prayed the date would turn out great.

We walked in and I was blown away. I had never been to an upscale restaurant before, let alone one that spun every few minutes. The most I had been used to was Papadeux (rolls eyes) so this was a whole new experience for me. I carried my head high and showed no emotion, I couldn't let him see how impressed I was. As we approached our table, he pulled out my chair and I thought *"wow, he's young, fly and the perfect gentleman"* and I couldn't get over the way he smelled, it was nothing like I had ever smelled before. If wealth had a smell, it would be him literally. It was turning me on from across the table. He ordered a bottle of champagne as we started the night by getting to know each other.

The date was going great, we were on our second bottle of champagne, and I didn't want the night to end. We had so much in common, I felt so lucky. He asked if I was single, and I said yes. Even though I still shared an apartment with Dami, our relationship was officially over, and nothing was getting in the way of this new relationship. We finished our dinner and headed back to mine as he would be dropping me off. As we approached my house, I thanked him for the best night ever and before I finished getting the words out, he leaned in for a kiss. It was the softest, yet juiciest kiss ever, *please don't let it end,* I prayed. But before I could catch myself, he pulled away. I walked upstairs still feeling the softness of his lips.

Days went by and my interaction with Papa intensified while Dami and I had fully cut all communication. I knew he was eventually going to show up to the house and I dreaded that day. Friday approached and Papa had asked me to accompany him to Belvedere and I agreed. I got ready and waited for him to pick me up. I was so excited. As we walked in and sat in our section, he poured my glass before his friends joined us. Midway through the night I spotted Dami staring at me with a look of disgust on his face. He had caught me red handed in the club dancing on Papa. *Oh no,* that was awkward but to be honest I didn't care.

While standing across from me Dami kept calling my phone and he watched as I declined the call each time. He eventually barged into our section demanding to speak to me. I was so embarrassed, so I acted like I didn't know who he was. I told them he had clearly mistaken me for someone else and he was thrown out. At the end of the night, I knew Dami would be home waiting for me to return so I decided to follow Papa home and we ended up having sex.

Two weeks into the relationship I moved in with Papa. We were in love; we were inseparable and insatiable. It got so bad his friends started hating me because I had stolen their friend away. They tried everything to end the relationship before it got even more serious but to no avail. He had become obsessed with me. Papa was pretty popular, so that boosted my popularity as well and before we knew it we had become Bonnie and Clyde.

As we sat in a restaurant eating dinner it occurred to me, I never asked Papa what he did for a living. He had all this money he was spending on me, yet I had never seen him get up to go to work. We were at home all day eating and making love or partying, so there's absolutely no way he worked for someone. "*How the hell do you make your money, put me on*" I asked. When it came to money matters, I never held my tongue, I was always bold and ready to make a check, he laughed and said he owned a business. But from the way he stuttered

I knew he was lying; I could tell because he couldn't look me in the eye. I asked again, but this time demanded the truth. Because Papa was such a pure hearted person. He decided to confess. *Do you really wanna know the truth? Can you handle the truth?* He asked. *Bring it on.* I replied. He laughed and said he would rather show me than tell me.

Papa was a yahoo boy and so were his friends. A yahoo boy is known as a fraudster, scammer or con artist, in short anyone with the intention to dupe someone out of their money or possessions. Over the next couple of years, I got sucked into a life of quick money schemes. We started doing petty jobs here and there that would pay us not more than $3,000 a job and before I knew it we had escalated into jobs paying us $10,000 a piece. From a girl working and making $500 a paycheck I was pocketing anywhere between $5,000-$10,000 daily and eventually quit my job. I had found a more lucrative means to sustain myself and because I stayed with Papa I had no bills to pay. I was finally free from that bondage they called a job and now I was living life on the edge and in the fast lane.

We began connecting with other fraudsters. One thing led to another, and we had boys willing to work for us. We recruited a team and could now relax and enjoy the money coming in. Our lifestyle became too expensive with the mediocre jobs we were pulling. We partied every night, shopped in designer stores and ate at all the upscale restaurants in the city. We needed more money to sustain our new habits. Papa would go out searching for fraudsters whenever we hit the clubs and he would always find, we started dealing with men bringing in hundreds of thousands of dollars, and this time our mode of operandi changed. It had become riskier, and I was at the forefront of it all. Papa and I were way in over our heads. We had every fraudster in the city calling us to help pull off their jobs, we took the term Bonnie and Clyde to a whole new level.

May 21st, 2014, a deposit of $150,000 had been wired into my account and they insisted I go to the bank to withdraw at least half of those funds. Being the naïve girl I was, and Papa not really knowing the ropes insisted I followed their instructions, so I did. I drove to the bank and requested a cash withdrawal of $25,000 and a cashier's check of $80,000 per their request. Due to shortage of funds at that location the teller was able to release only $10,000 in cash and asked me to return the next day when the money would be available. Papa had been so eager to impress these guys that he damned the risk, and me trusting him I went along with his idea even though I had a bad feeling about this job.

Morning came around and we both got dressed and headed to the bank. This time Papa followed me inside to assist me. Something must have seemed off because as I approached the teller from the day before and she put up an attitude and asked me to wait for the manager. He came out and took us into his office to ask what we were planning to do with all that money, and we answered diligently. He handed us a piece of paper and asked us to call a number to speak to a particular agent who had flagged the account due to fraudulent activity. In a fury we stormed out of the bank, rushed home and called the agent, *"why is my money and my account being placed on hold by you sir?"* I asked, and he replied with numerous questions about why I had received the transfer and what I had planned to use the money to purchase. I kept lying through my teeth and something deep down inside of me told me he wasn't buying any of my stories.

Papa on the other hand had been on the phone dealing with his business associates as they had become demanding for their funds. Papa explained to them our predicament, but they weren't hearing any of it. *"Babe I think we should free this money; I don't know what's going on, but it looks suspicious,"* I said to Papa. He shushed me and assured me we would get it.

Days passed and these men continuously demanded for all their money claiming we were trying to play a fast one on them, even after they had heard the numerous phone calls to this agent.

On May 31st, 2014, it all came crashing down before my eyes. A couple days before my birthday I had woken up from what seemed to be a nightmare, but it felt so real. In my dream I had been arrested on my birthday by a Caucasian man in a suit and all I could remember was that I was crying nonstop. I woke up in a pool of sweat, the dream felt too close to home, I could almost feel it. That morning as I woke up Papa asked me to call the agent again and to my surprise as he picked up first thing he said was *"you are free to go pick up your money"* I thought to myself this was too good to be true and after the dream I just had, there was no way I was touching that money. Papa and I argued for hours until he finally persuaded me, He convinced me that even after picking up the money, we would spend it all on my birthday. We made plans to go to Las Vegas and ball out, so with this extra money I could only imagine the shopping I would do.

My little cousin at the time had come over to visit and we all set out to the bank, little did I know that something was going to go wrong. My cousin and Papa sat in the car waiting while I hurried into the bank thinking the money was packed up and ready for my collection. Upon entering the bank I was asked to wait in the office until they counted every single note. I waited for about 30 minutes until an officer walked up to me and asked me what I had come to do in the bank, and before I knew it my hands were behind my back. I was searched and taken to the back of the police van. Out of fear of his own safety papa drove off with my cousin, and just like my dream I was arrested and spent my birthday in jail.

*****

The four days I spent in jail were the longest four days of my life, four days not knowing if I would ever get out or see daylight again. I blamed Papa, but at the same time blamed myself for being so stupid. On the outside Papa was panicking and so were his associates, they feared I would snitch on them and quickly changed all their phone numbers. Some even fled the city immediately. They let Papa bear the guilt and responsibility of getting me out of jail alone. So, he did what he thought was best.

I was released on the 4th of June 2014, the night of my birthday when I least expected it. God had clearly been speaking to me, but I refused to listen to him and change my ways. As we got home, I asked Papa how he managed to get me released and he told me not to worry that it was handled, and I would never have to live through that again. Well, he was wrong. My first appearance in court was a few days later and I had skipped out on court because Papa said I didn't have to show up as he had bonded me out with a fake name and since I was arrested with a different name they would never know; we were dumb and very wrong. A warrant was issued for my arrest immediately.

Exactly a month later I was re-arrested outside a restaurant we were eating at by a bounty hunter and I spent the next two weeks in county jail. Upon getting booked, I was tested and evaluated and that was when I discovered I was carrying Papa's child. "*Not this shit again*, I thought" I was too devastated to care about the pregnancy, I had just been denied bail due to me skipping out on the last one so to my best knowledge I was going to become a sitting duck waiting for whenever they decided to try my case.

I became depressed, and all I wanted to do was sleep. I got tired of calling Papa as he never had any positive news for me and even though he would try to cheer me up I could hear the despair in his voice. His uncertainty made me sadder. I eventually stopped calling him and accepted my faith.

In lockup I had a bedmate who slept above me, her name was Tarrika, but everyone called her T. She was considered an O.G. She had been in and out of jail almost all her life and racked up an extensive rap sheet of charges from possession and intent to sell, to trafficking, prostitution, and gun charges. You name it and she had gone to jail for it. The guards all seemed to have been fond of her as she was a regular, so she had a couple favors and added perks. She walked around like she owned the place, and everyone respected her, lucky me right! She grew a liking to me and always assured me I would be out in no time as my crime was childish, she gave me the ins and outs and the rundown of every girl in lock up with me.

Over the next few days, I learnt a lot about my fellow inmates, their charges and the reasons behind their life of crimes. Sigh, life has been hard on some people. Always be grateful for the life you have because some people's stories will have you too scared to sleep at night. Their stories gave me hope, something to look forward to and I grew to love them. The depression of being pregnant in jail still held me down and because of how picky I am with food I survived off sliced buttered bread and milk alone.

Everyone knew I only ate bread so girls would come and trade their bread for my meals and eventually I started getting their meds for my meals. One day T said to me *"I have something that will make you feel good",*

What is it? I asked.

She brought out a pill from the back of her tongue and handed it to me, *eww did she expect me to swallow her wet pill?* Yup she did, and that's exactly what I did. That pill had me asleep for two days straight only waking up to grab my lunch. That was the best thing anyone could have given me in jail, and they kept giving it to me until I got out.

The night I got out of jail I informed Papa of my pregnancy and insisted I wanted it terminated by the end of the week. He was heartbroken but obliged. In the morning, we set out to get a checkup and that was where I found out I was having twins. Papa pleaded with me to keep his twins, unfortunately I refused and terminated them. We had started drifting apart slowly and I eventually learned he had cheated on me with my friend. Well, that was the straw that broke the camel's back. I broke up with him and moved out of the apartment. He came back begging. He called, sent me gifts and flowers but the truth was it wasn't the cheating alone. It was the fact I had become bored, the routine had become repetitive, and I silently resented him for costing me my freedom. I wanted freedom, I wanted out, and after three years I was back in the streets and on the prowl.

Tunde fast cash and Jide call back were Houston's most notorious scammers and playboys. They had the money, the girls and the lifestyle every girl wanted a piece of. They were best friends and business partners and literally lived like brothers, their bond was unbreakable. I had dealings with them in the past through Papa and we were cordial.

One night, my girls and I had our night out at a strip club. While in the club, I spotted Tunde and decided to storm his section. I had just gotten a Brazilian butt lift and my entire demeanor had changed. I had a confidence that was alluring, and I got anything and anyone I wanted. As I walked into his section, he immediately began pouring our drinks. Tunde knew of my past with Papa and that was what intrigued him about me, he wished for a girl like me. Someone he could trust and could hold it down, his ride or die. After learning Papa and I had split he set out to make me his woman. I was enjoying my new body and freedom too much to be tied down by any man, so I made him put in the work.

We partied almost every night and travelled to Miami a lot, at first it was just a sexual relationship, with no strings attached but we eventually grew feelings for each other. Tunde was adorable, rich and a little local, he had just moved into the states, and he was overwhelmed with the system. So, I was there to handle everything for him- his money, his personal needs and sexual needs. I was like his very own personal assistant - the ones that sleep with their bosses. Once again, I had been sucked into a world of parties and bullshit. We had started taking ecstasy together and it intensified our relationship. He did anything I wanted and gave me everything and for the time being he was perfect. Tunde had me lodged in different hotels in the city round the clock. He introduced me to a new life of luxury, and my friends and I enjoyed every bit of it.

Slowly I started catching feelings for Tunde, it became more than just sex and drugs for me, I wanted more. Even though I was the one who initially set the tone for our friendship I wanted a do over. Tunde, on the other hand, enjoyed having full access to me without the commitment. He was free to talk to any other female he desired, and I couldn't get angry, but deep down that frustrated me. I had made myself look so tough and I couldn't back down so instead I suffered in silence.

Tunde was a chronic womanizer, he chased everything and everyone in a skirt. Rumors of his womanizing ways had begun to spread, and I needed to separate myself from him. At that point I could no longer come out to claim him as mine because it would have been an embarrassment to me. I began to limit my public appearances with him and eventually cut him off when he started attempting to have sexual intercourse with my friend while I slept in his bed, how disrespectful!

On one night out in town, I walked into the strip club thinking Tunde would be there but instead I met Jide. Jide was a much older man, in his late thirties, average height with a pot belly. He was not my type in any way, but I knew how rich he was and his rank in the food chain, so I pursued. My initial plan was to work with him. I needed a new hustle because now I had to sort my bill since I was no longer with Tunde. Interestingly, Jide had his eyes set on me for a while, so he came prepared.

Over the next couple of days Jide became my knight in shining armor. Jide was experienced, he had been in the game longer and taught Tunde everything he knew, so he knew what to do and how to do it. I continued living in hotels courtesy of Jide and he made sure I never lacked anything. On nights I wanted to party he would have my table booked and drinks fully paid for. He flew me and my friends to any city of our choice and always had me in designer stores. I had finally hit the jackpot, so I thought.

Eventually the hotel life became draining, I wanted my own space and Jide got me a nice apartment in the heart of river oaks, the city's high-end neighborhood. In return, I would have to work for him, which I agreed to. He introduced me to some of his dealings and before I knew it, I was handling all his business. I became his main chick and he started stashing all his fraudulent documents at my apartment, safe to say my place became his safe house. Tunde heard of our new relationship and became extremely jealous. He tried everything possible to break Jide and I up.

I still continued my sexual adventure with Tunde, even though I was with Jide because sex with him was fun compared to Jide. Tunde became extremely jealous of his best friend and their enmity started, with Jide being left in the dark. For Tundes 33rd birthday he planned a week-long massive party in Miami for his friends. As his best friend's girlfriend, I had to tag along even though I knew how awkward it would be for the both of us.

Unfortunately, Tunde was arrested upon arrival into Miami and just like that our supposedly fun weekend became a nightmare. Jide fled Miami leaving me there to sort his best friend out. When Tunde realized how his best friend abandoned him, he became furious and swore to destroy him. Their friendship turned sour overnight. Jide was unaware of a lot of things until I told him everything. I told him how his best friend felt about him dating me and how he really felt about their friendship.

Jide was dumbfounded, he couldn't believe what he was hearing. *"How could Tunde be jealous of us? He made a bet with me that I couldn't have u and I won"*

What? Those words broke me, not because the guy I had grown to really like made a bet over me, but because he clearly held me to high standards, and I failed him. I blew it. At that point Jide and I individually realized that Tunde had more feelings for me than he was letting out. He wanted more than the initial arrangement we had, but for the same reason I couldn't request for more, he couldn't. In that space I knew I had created a big mess and over time it became messier. It had become a full-on tug of war and I was stuck in the middle of it.

My heart was still with Tunde, but I had unbreakable ties with Jide, there was too much at stake for me to walk away. I had become indebted to Jide and I needed him to survive. Overtime, their misunderstanding became a full-on blood bath. They fought every time they crossed each other's path and it always ended badly. One night during one of their crazy fights outside the club, Tunde pulled a gun and hit Jide on the head. The place immediately became a crazy scene when people saw the gun; everyone started running helter skelter. Someone called the police, and luckily for Jide he quickly regained consciousness and escaped.

As much as the fights involved just the both of them, it worried me so much and after a while I started feeling the heat too. One time, Tunde paid some notorious gangsters in Houston to kidnap and beat Jide and I up. Fortunately for us, one of the gangsters was a friend's ex-boyfriend. Out of the kindness of his heart, he told me about the plan. I immediately told Jide who found a way around it and was able to resolve it. When Tunde saw that he was not able to hurt Jide enough, He went to the police to snitch on him. This was very bad for Jide because he was already a man of interest with the police. They had been searching for him for a while but unluckily for Tunde, Jide was able to resolve that.

Now that Jide was temporarily off the hook, the fights started all over again. It became really messy and I was stuck in between. I didn't know what to do or who to run to. Tunde was determined to destroy Jide and kept looking for new ways. Jide, on the other hand, was determined to show Tunde that he was the boss and more dangerous. Tunde went back to the police again but this time around, he was unlucky because he encountered an FBI agent who had been trailing the both of them. The agent arrested them but somehow Tunde ran away and fled the country leaving Jide to face jail time. And that was the last I heard of them.

Chapter 9

Lagos!

Even though the whole mess had cleared up, I was still very scared. I was romantically and financially involved with these two men and now that one of them was in custody, what was my fate? I feared getting arrested again, who would help me this time? I had absolutely no one I could count on. One day I decided I was going to purchase a plane ticket and fly back to Nigeria to cool off until things die down in Houston. I needed a new means to make money, because I had used up all my savings.

I called one of my friends In Nigeria and explained my predicament. She laughed and said *you better book your ticket quickly and get down here and let's have some fun.* Well, that's exactly what I did. After so many years I booked a plane ticket and headed for Nigeria. The feeling was bittersweet, I didn't know what to expect, I didn't have a plan, I was just going where the wind blew me. I landed in Lagos and the heat and smell that welcomed me was discouraging. The confusion and unprofessionalism left me in a state of disbelief. At some point all the lights in the airport went off and the whole place was pitch black. I was terrified.

I had no recollection of what the country looked like, but from the little I could remember the state of the country had gotten worse just by the look of the airport. I immediately pondered *"what I could possibly gain from this country"*. Before my arrival, my friend introduced me to a guy named Wale Roberts. We had been chatting for a couple of weeks and had gotten quite familiar with each other. I told him I was coming to Lagos, and he sent his security detail to pick me up. As I approached the airport exit, I saw my friend Tina standing there with his police escort waiting for me. We were so excited to see each other and literally jumped into each other's arms. We spent some minutes exchanging pleasantries before we proceeded to the car park. When we entered the car, she handed me a key to my hotel room, a presidential suite at Eko signature hotel, one of those most expensive and exclusive hotels in Lagos at the time. All expenses fully paid for by Wale Roberts.

This is getting interesting, I thought

Wale Roberts was the last son of an ex-governor, and a very prominent and powerful politician in Nigeria. He appeared humble but from his choice of words I could tell he was a spoilt brat who had everything. From riches and power to access to all the state's powerful leaders. He was the city's most eligible bachelor or should I say playboy. In his late twenties he had spent most of his life in London and recently returned to Nigeria to shadow his father. He was wild and everyone wanted a piece of him.

After sitting in traffic for over three hours we finally arrived at Eko hotel. I was tired and exhausted, all I wanted at that moment was a cold bath. The reception at the hotel was amazing, we were ushered into our room and were given everything we needed. Since I left the airport, I had not been able to access the internet so the moment I settled in and connected to the Wi-Fi I got a message from him saying *"TGIF, welcome back babe get ready, I'll come pick you up in an hour and we will hit the town"*.

I hopped in the shower and began to get ready for the night. Being a woman, my one hour turned into two hours. Before I was done, he had been waiting for me downstairs for over thirty minutes. He was parked in front of the hotel with a five-car entourage which consisted of two police escort vehicles, his assistant in one car, friends in the other, and his convertible which I jumped in. It was midnight and I was exhausted, but my night was just beginning. He insisted we grab a bite to eat first as the night would be long and there would be serious alcohol involved. We arrived at Bungalow restaurant. He insisted on going there because he said it was his favorite spot for cocktails and they made the best pepperoni pizza. It was like he read my mind because that was just what I had been craving, a hot cheesy pepperoni pizza. The pizza was okay but not comparable to the one in the states. We took a couple shots and headed to our next destination- Sip nightclub, in the heart of Victoria Island. We walked in holding hands, we were acting all mush and sweet, no one would have known we just met a couple hours ago. Maybe it was the alcohol we had earlier setting in, because cocktails in Nigeria are a bit stronger.

As we walked into our section the drinks came almost immediately like they had been awaiting our arrival. We were only about four people in the section, excluding his bodyguard, yet the drinks were so many- five bottles of champagne, two bottles of Hennessey and two bottles of vodka, I thought to myself *"who is this man trying to kill"* I had no intention of getting that drunk.

As we progressed into the night, I began noticing how quickly those bottles were finishing and yes, we were the ones drinking them. We danced like there was no tomorrow. I had gotten so drunk I didn't know where I was or what was going on anymore, but I was having the time of my life. I fell in love with Wale on that night. Eventually we had enough, we were all wasted, and I was almost dozing at some point. I needed sleep, I was still jet lagged from my trip and my alcohol level must have been way past the legal limit. We knew we had to get out of there quickly or they would end up carrying us out of there ha-ha. We stumbled and staggered to the car with the guidance of his bodyguard and once we got in the car we passed out. *What a match made in heaven right?*

As we approached my hotel, one of his guards tapped my leg and said, *"madam we have arrived at your hotel, will you be coming down or following us home?"* All I heard was hotel. I leaned forward, grabbed my purse and shoes I had kicked off and looked at Wale, he was knocked out. I kissed his cheek and walked into the hotel and up to my room barefooted, the rest of the night was a blur. Waking up the next day, I checked my phone, and it was already afternoon. I had only gotten five hours of sleep, I was groggy, exhausted, dehydrated and left with a mean hangover. I went into the bathroom to freshen up, while in the bathroom, my phone rang. It was Wale was on the line. I jumped up with excitement and hurried to pick up.

How are you? He asked

I'm wasted, can you believe I just woke up

Me too. He replied laughing *Damn, we had a really crazy night. I didn't even know when you left the car*

I saw that you were sleeping and didn't want to bother you. To be honest, I don't know how I got to this room. All I know is that I woke up on the bed.

Maybe you teleported. He said laughing. *Get ready, I am coming to pick you up in an hour. Let your one hour be one house o*

Don't worry, I will try.

As excited as I was to be seeing him again, I feared being too hungover to function, "*I hope I don't come off as a bitch*" I thought.

He always kept to time, if he said an hour, he was sure to be there at exactly the time he stated, it was a major plus for him. I jumped in his car, and we headed out to the restaurant. We had a nice chat in the car and talked about a lot of things. Unlike last night when I was too tired, I had a bit of strength, so I engaged him in conversations. We pulled up to the Golden Gate Chinese restaurant and it was like this guy was a psychic. How could he possibly know all the things I loved; it was obvious my friend had given him the 411.

As we settled in, I texted her asking her if she gave this guy the cheat code and she assured me she didn't. *Wow how cool I can't believe I found a keeper in Nigeria.* My friend on the other hand became jealous, I had totally abandoned her for this guy and that was not the plan. Immediately we sat down, he ordered a bottle of champagne and some patron shots. *woah, woah, woah are you trying to kill me?* I asked, "*everyone knows the best way to get rid of a hangover is to drink more alcohol*" as he chuckled, I knew this guy was going to be serious trouble for me.

We began drinking all over again and ended up drunk. We headed back to the hotel and all I could think of on our way there was how bad I wanted to kiss him. The feeling was mutual because the moment we got in the room, he grabbed me and kissed me. It was passionate and I felt every nerve in my body responding to his touch as we made out. We were about to get down when he said *"let's save this for later, right now I want you to change let's hit the streets"*

Okayyyy??? I thought. I loved the arrogance; I loved the confidence. Clearly, I had a type and it had nothing to do with looks. I quickly changed and we ran back out. We went back to the same night club and did the same thing all over but this time we both had something to look out for- the sex we would have later. We could not keep our hands off each other all through the night. The moment we got into the room, we let loose, we took our clothes off within seconds. We were like animals let out of a zoo. As I began undressing, he smiled at me, with his fist closed and reached out towards me, *'you want some, you do this?'*

Not Cocaine again, I thought. I stood there with a stupid smile on my face hoping that somehow it would just play itself out and I wouldn't have to give him an answer but the words that came out of my mouth surprised me, *"hell yeah, just what I needed"* I cannot believe I just accepted to do cocaine.

My heart started beating fast as he began setting up on the table beside me, a million thoughts going through my mind, *what if this is the day I die right in front of this guy, what is he going to do? What if I have a bad trip and I do or say something weird, and he realizes I have never done this before then I'll look like lame ugh.* It was a loose-loose situation, and I couldn't handle the pressure. I ensured my facial expression remained calm; I couldn't let him see me panicking.

As he lined up the cocaine on the table, he rolled up a $100 dollar bill and handed it to me. I laughed and handed it right back and said, *"you go first"*. He probably thought I was being cautious about what I would be snorting in when I just wanted to mimic how he was snorting it. I learnt all I need to learn in .5 seconds. As I leaned forward, I quickly said a prayer in my head *"Lord pls don't let me die, I'm sorry"* and snorted the first line. I was still alive, I was still breathing, I was still normal. *Whew that was close*, I said, thinking it would be the end of that, but it was just the beginning.

We ended up doing lines for hours unending, we were high as kites and at this point, I was ready to go to bed. I honestly couldn't tell what the cocaine had done to me except make me extremely sleepy and agitated. I began to yawn and eventually walked over to the bed and laid down. Once he realized how sleepy I was he ran over to continue the make out session. I had lost the passion I had earlier, I just wanted to sleep but I played along. We went on for hours trying to get him erect but it wasn't working, *what's wrong?* I asked, *"coke dick duh"* he replied, I could hear the despair in his response as we continued trying until he finally got it up.

First thing in the morning, he got up and left. I woke up feeling like a truck had hit me the night. I was tired and beyond exhausted. My body felt so heavy and my head was pounding. I texted him saying I needed space to recuperate. I hated what he made me do. That was a door I wanted to remain closed but here I was, the third day in Lagos with a clogged nostril, a double hangover and puffy eyes. I came here to relax, not to have a cardiac arrest. I need to get away from this guy. I texted my friend and told her what happened, she laughed and asked if she could come over. *Pls move in with me*, I asked, so she did.

Tina was my tour guide in Lagos, she knew everyone's business, but they never really knew her, why? She spent most of her days on Facebook stalking the cool kids, she had info on anyone you could think of from young to old, she had the tea. She always knew the parties to attend and places to go to meet people. Although Tina was my friend, she was a wannabe, and everyone knew it. Her desperation to belong, to fit in, to be seen was so glaring. With me by her side she had bargaining power. The people she so desperately wanted to fit in with had begun noticing her because they wanted to know who the new American girl was.

One day we were invited to a house party, and that was where I met Lawrence. He was blatantly rude, and cocky but so damn fine. We didn't know who his father was, but he had died and left him a fortune. He was a super-rich kid and somehow, we had been invited to his birthday party, and we just so happened to be the youngest girls at the party. Our first encounter with him was terrible, he was so nasty to my friend that it left me speechless. I had never seen a guy so mannerless and for some reason it turned me on.

Lawrence began talking to me trying to get to know me and although I was a bit skeptical due to his rude behavior, I kept the convo going. I was about seven years younger than he was, but he didn't mind getting to know me. From the first night I met Lawrence I was intimidated, because of how he spoke to my friend. It was obvious he had an interest in me so I told him before we could proceed, he had to apologize to my friend. *It will amaze you what men will do for sex.*

I was afraid of how rude Lawrence was, he came off as a guy that would embarrass me, so I kept it cool with him. I played hard to get. I was still seeing Wale sometimes, but he was too much to handle. The drugs, the alcohol, the sex, it was just too much for me, so I started limiting our interactions, but he always seemed to pop up wherever I was. Lagos is a big city, but the circles run so small, it was almost impossible not bumping into him and every time we locked eyes, he would text me saying *"you are leaving with me"*. I couldn't turn him down, he was my baby, and he was also paying for my room, so we ended up walking out together every time.

Wale had exposed me to the wild side of life, I started doing cocaine more often with him; we were living young, wild and free. One night as we left the club, he ditched his security guards so he could drive himself. As we sped down the streets of Ikoyi, high and out of our minds, he pulled his pants down while driving and requested I give him a blowjob. The thrill of it blew my mind, this guy had me doing wild things. We drove straight to his family house and jumped in the pool where we had sex. Wale was a wild person who got a thrill off doing extreme things and he liked me so much because I was willing to do it all with no questions asked. Over time he exposed me to so many drugs and alcohol. We were high all the time. One day he said *"let's make a sex tape"*. I was terrified and deep down didn't want to, but at this point I was willing to do anything and everything he asked of me. I enjoyed being his woman, and nothing was going to break us up.

On the other hand, Lawrence and I kept talking. We would often bump into each other at the club and anytime I saw him, he always had a girl on his arm. However, we always stole glances at each other the entire night, I thought it was cute. I wanted Lawrence too, but

Wale and Lawrence rolled in the same tight circle. There was no way I could pull it off. I did every nasty thing you could think of with Wale, from snorting cocaine out of my private part to my first foursome with two other girls, to random sex in weird places. We once had sex in the club bathroom while his security guard watched the doors so no one could enter. We were on a wild ride and one day it came crashing down right before my eyes.

One night, I declined his invite to go out because my friends weren't sure they wanted to party. We had been partying all week long and we honestly needed a break, he agreed and said he would also be staying in as well because he had work in the morning. We said our goodnights and hung up the call. Couple hours later, Tina decided we should go to Aura nightclub because someone she had been eyeing was there and she needed to get closer to him. We got dressed and hit the streets. As we approached the entrance of the club, I saw Wale walking out with a girl holding his hands, the same way we held hands.

My heart began beating fast as I approached them. As they walked past me, he smiled, and leaned in to kiss my cheek then whispered, *"I'll see you later babe"*. wow the audacity. I had never been so embarrassed by a man before; I froze and by the time I snapped out of it I was filled with rage. I began walking towards them to confront them when Tina pushed me forward and said, *"if you like yourself, then you better not attempt what I think you're trying too, this is Lagos, he runs this city"* and she pulled me back towards her direction. I spent the entire night sulking over Wale, thinking about how he was doing the same things he did with me to her. I had just experienced my first Lagos heartbreak.

I woke up the next morning and decided Wale was a thing of the past, and I decided to move on. Lawrence was my new target, I called him up and we made plans to meet up later. With Lawrence I had been playing hard to get because I was skeptical about him. He knew his worth, and it made him very arrogant towards women, so I treaded lightly. We met up at a restaurant, had a couple drinks and he dropped me off at my hotel. We hung out a couple times and partied a few times too. I noticed Lawrence wasn't the romantic type, nor was he looking for a serious relationship, he was enjoying the single life and not even I would change that.

I refused to have any form of sexual encounter with Lawrence because I didn't want it ending the way it ended with Wale. I was too emotional, and I grew attachments easily, so it was better to keep it platonic. Lawrence hated the fact that I wasn't eager to sleep with him like all the other girls who he had in rotation. I just wanted to party and have a good time with my girls. He couldn't understand why I wasn't fazed by his antics, and it drove him crazy, because he could see I wasn't impressed. Wale had taught me a valuable lesson about men in Lagos. And with Tina constantly hammering it in me that *"Lagos men would embarrass you"* I knew I had to play safe.

Lawrence had officially started pressuring me for sex indirectly, he would attempt to take me home with the promises of us sleeping in different rooms, yeah right! Eventually I gave into the pressure, and we had sex. My first thought was *"with all his arrogance I thought he would blow my mind"*. To be honest it wasn't bad, but it wasn't great either, I could live without it. After the first time we had sex, I knew we would only remain friends, but the extent of our friendship is what I hadn't given much thought to. Lawrence tried to hook up with me more than often, but I constantly dodged him. Every time he met at the club, he would grab me and pull me out with him until we got to his place.

He never took no for an answer, he never respected my wishes. He would walk in with a girl and walk out with me in his arms. I never wanted to go with him, but I did not know how to refuse him at the same time. A part of me feared him, and he knew it. Eventually I had enough, I was tired of the mediocre sex, I was tired of going by what he wanted, I was tired of having my plans ruined by him, so I started avoiding him. From then on, anytime he walked into any club I was in, I would duck and dive till I successfully sneak out. Tina became tired of having to leave in the middle of her turn up because of Lawrence so one day she refused, and I had no choice but stay. Lawrence walked up to me and said *"grab your bag let's go home"*

I stood up to him for the first time and responded *"umm, I don't remember coming here with you, so I'm not leaving with you"*. He chuckled then grabbed me by the arm and dragged me out of the club with everyone staring at us. I was so embarrassed I couldn't breathe. It was official, he had started bullying me.

All the while he was pulling me, I was trying to get my hand off, but I couldn't until we got outside. Then I lost it and started yelling at him *"you can't keep controlling me like that, you're not my dad"*. I turned to walk back in but the bouncer at the door denied me access. I turned back in confusion and saw Lawrence laughing, he then said *"it's either we leave together, or you stand outside the club and wait for everyone to come out and meet you here. Choose"*. At this point I was furious and demanded that the bouncer let me in, but he blatantly denied me access. At one point he told me *"oga Lawrence said no entry for you"* I had been defeated once again, and once again I ended up in his bed.

We continued like this for months, and one day I left his house in the morning and blocked him. He was to have no access to me whatsoever. I needed a break from him. I hated anyone restricting my freedom and not only was he restricting my freedom, but he was also bullying me into giving him sex. I stayed indoors for the next couple of days and when my girls and I finally decided to paint the town red, we hit up our favorite spot first - Sip nightclub. It was for the cool kids and the DJ always knew what we loved to hear. We met with a couple of Tina's male friends and sat with them. As I turned to the left, two tables beside us were Lawrence and his friends, my heart began beating fast as he stared at me.

To my surprise for the first time, he didn't walk up to me, even though I could sense his anger from the way he stared at me. I also refused to keep eye contact. That night I drank so much that I forgot he was a couple tables away from me, he watched me flirt with so many guys he couldn't handle it anymore, so he walked over to me and demanded to talk to me. I refused but he began making a scene and in order to avoid that embarrassment I followed him outside. He began yelling at me while I stood there confused, *"is this guy insane?" I wasn't even his girlfriend, and he was commanding me like that"*. At that very moment I realized I didn't have to explain anything to him and attempted to walk off mid conversation when he pulled me back and slapped me *"how dare you walk away, are you crazy, am I your mate?"*. I froze, I was left standing there in utter disbelief as he pulled my arm and dragged me back into the club. Wow, no man had ever slapped me before, let alone a man I wasn't even committed to. As we got upstairs and walked to his table, he sat me down right beside him while I watched him dance and party with the girls he came out with. At the end of the night, we went home together and had sex like nothing happened.

I just knew I had bitten more than I could chew with Lawrence and if I didn't put a stop to the madness, it would only get worse. As I left his house that morning and got back to my hotel room, I woke Tina up with tears in my eyes and told her the story. She laughed in my face and said, *"good for you, maybe now you can leave all these boys alone and make money"*. She was right, I came to Nigeria to make money but rather I had only gotten my heart and cheekbone broken.

I decided to boss up, none of these guys would get in my way again. I had my eyes on the prize, whatever that meant, and I wasn't letting up. Lagos turned me into a party girl, I was in the clubs every single day of the week from sunup to sundown. Alcohol and drugs became my coping mechanism. I had completely lost my sense of self; I had completely immersed myself into a world I couldn't get out of. I began losing sight of what I really wanted out of life and surrounded myself with a bunch of people who had no lives. Friends as they would call it.

One day Tina came back from her night out and started ranting about how she was insulted by a man. She was so pissed and decided to become a millionaire, 'a boss bitch' in her words. She went on and on about how money was the solution to her problems, and I couldn't agree more. She devised a plan- one that had me a bit worried. She said she needed to do jazz for favor. I thought what in the hell was she talking about. She pulled out a magazine, as we flipped through the pages, she showed me an ad and said *'let me call him'*. The ad read *"if you're looking for favor, wealth, love charm, protection contact us today"*. I waited for her to get off the phone to explain to me what was going on. Instead she hung up and acted like it was a joke while avoiding my question. I thought *"Tina always has something going on"*. She was all over the place, always indecisive and last minute so I assumed this was just another Tina moment, but I was wrong.

First thing Wednesday morning, Tina woke up and began packing her things, *"where are you going?"* I asked and she said *"oh I must go home immediately, I have a couple errands I have to run for my mom"* I thought nothing of it because she would always head home from time to time to check on her house, so I went back to bed.

Tina returned after four days of being incommunicado. *Where have you been? Why couldn't I reach you?* I asked

"Oh, my phone broke on my way home. I just picked it up from the repair guy on

my way here and I'm tired I need to sleep". I could tell something was off, it was unlike her to disappear for four days with no communication. I knew she was lying but I just couldn't place my finger on what she was lying about.

Over the next few days she became so sneaky and dodgy, and I knew she was up to something. As she left the hotel one night to meet up with a male companion, she had agreed to have dinner with, I double bolted the hotel door and began searching her belongings. I searched and searched but found nothing and as I was attempting to put everything back, a little black baggy fell to the ground. It looked weird, so I began opening it up. Inside this small bag was a little object wrapped in a tiny piece of red clothing. As I continued unwrapping it, I started feeling the object get hotter and hotter until I eventually threw it on the floor and watched it turn to black ash. As i dropped it, I realized it burned my finger. I was terrified, *what could that have been?*

I sat down and waited for her to return. As she returned from her date, I immediately confronted her and demanded an explanation. *Tina, I found something in your bag and as I touched it, I got burnt.* As I pointed to what was left of it on the floor, she freaked out and started panicking, *oh my God Amanda, why will you touch my stuff? Are you crazy? I'm ruined, I'm going to run mad.* She said as she almost started crying. At this point I was slightly hesitant to know what she meant by me ruining her life because I felt like the least, I knew, the better for me. After hours of panting up and down the room in a state of duress she finally sat down and agreed to explain her ordeal to me.

A friend of hers took her to see some popular man in Ogun state known for helping all the runz girls in Lagos gain favor and riches from men. This man was popular for putting together charms that would bring good luck to any woman that sought after him for a small price. She and her friends set out to a forest in Ogun state where they met the man. Upon meeting him, he asked them to strip off their clothing and tie only a white towel during the entire process which they did. She said they were individually asked what their hearts desired, and they all stated money. The man told them they would all have to pay a sum of fifty thousand naira and return the next day to perform the rituals, which they did.

Tina said as they returned, they met three much older women with the man, dressed in red towels and with white markings on their body, so they became a little scared. On approaching they were asked to strip again but this time with no towel. The man told them that they needed to perform the ritual with a virgin girl, and he had brought the girl out for them. He had the girl lay unconscious on the floor while he and his assistants walked round her chanting incantations. Once he was done each of the girls were to stand over her reciting the same incantations. Tina said while she was standing over the girl, she woke up and began crying. The man blew something on her, which made her fall asleep again until they finished performing the rituals.

For the second part of the ritual, they had to stand in a circle around a big basket and just like magic, money in all currencies and denominations started appearing in the basket, all they had to do was pick the bills out. They picked and picked for hours and upon completion they had to spend the night in that forest. The next day he instructed them to come back and collect the charms he had prepared for each of them. She said he also emphasized that it be kept in secret and not touched by anyone else, a charm I had not only seen and touched but threw on the floor and destroyed it.

On hearing this story, I was shocked. I couldn't believe her, and I didn't want to. I couldn't phantom the idea that Tina was so desperate she would go through such a daunting task. However, from her reaction to the charm being on the floor there had to be some truth to it right?

Chapter 10

P!

What is P? It is the acronym for parole. What is parole you ask? To many, it is considered a quick money scheme, or shall I say a quick hookup for sex. One minute you're at home, next minute you're on your way to have a quickie with someone you have never met. Sometimes you might even be getting on a jet to go see a governor based on your pictures being approved. Almost every girl in Lagos has either heard of the term p or somehow been involved in it.

My first experience with P was with an older man named Yusef, he owned a guesthouse on the island that my friends and I frequented. One day while exiting the building, a car pulled up in front of my friend Tina and she began talking to a man. We left her behind and proceeded to wait for her in the taxi. After about 10 minutes Tina approached us with a big smile on her face and as we questioned her about the conversation she had. She pulled out a wad of cash from her purse, *"Amanda this is for you, it is from the man I was talking too"*

what for? I asked,

He said he liked you and he wanted to buy you lunch and extend your room as he was the owner of the building. She replied with a smirk on her face.

Aww nice I said as I collected the money out of her hand and put it in my purse.

Tina continued to talk about the man all day as if she were slowly forcing me into agreeing to meet him. After my experience with Ben, I had not had any contact with an older married man and Yusef would be my first.

Tina called Yusef immediately after we got back to the guesthouse after our errands for the day. He was in our room within 20 minutes of calling him. Here was this old man sitting on the couch beside my bed staring at me with lust in his eyes while Tina introduced us. Yusef was repulsive and vulgar, he was so used to girls flocking around him and bowing to his every demand that when he met me, he was intrigued by my stubbornness. I was probably the first girl he had encountered that didn't really care for his antics. He constantly begged me to be his girlfriend and I constantly refused.

On this day Tina and I had our friend Sharon over. As we watched TV and caught up on old times we heard a knock on the door, it was Yusef, and he was drunk, very drunk. He barged into my room and said he wanted to join in on our little fun, but we refused stating how late it was. Tina tried to get him to leave but instead he pulled out a bundle of foreign currency and said, *"it's all for her if she sleeps with me tonight"*. As Tina spotted the money her jaw dropped. She quickly offered him a seat; it was as if a light bulb switched on in her head. I was pissed at his audacity and immediately said no and proceeded to leave the room. She looked at me with a smirk on her face as I said no and pulled me into the bathroom.

"Amanda think about this, look at all that money he's willing to give you, it's just sex and besides he's drunk it probably won't last more than five minutes" she said. I blatantly refused, no way in hell was I going to sleep with this dirt bag, he made my skin crawl. Tina knelt down on one knee and held my hands and started begging me with almost tears in her eyes, *"please Amanda I really need this money, you need it too but I need it the most and besides you messed up my jazz now I'm screwed, you at least owe it to me"*. I felt pity for her and for a moment I started to reconsider. At this point she had successfully guilt tripped me into agreeing but I had one condition, they would have to join me to make it more comfortable. I walked out of the bathroom and blurted out to Yusef *"I will sleep with you after you sleep with both of my friends first"*. He nodded in agreement. As a man he was getting a three for one special, and they both took turns individually sleeping with him.

What they didn't know was I had a plan- a well thought out plan. I knew how drunk he was, and he seemed exhausted so I thought to myself that if they went first by the time, he had finished with them he would barely have energy for me. But I was wrong, something weird happened. When it got to my turn I undressed and joined him in the bed while my friends waited in the bathroom for us to finish. As I laid in the bed, he got on top of me and from the look of fear in my face he could tell I wasn't one bit interested, so he whispered in my ear *"I'm not going to force you to have sex with me, but since you have an agreement, we need to pretend, so moan"*. I obeyed and for 10 minutes he moved around on top of me in a thrusting position while I moaned as realistically as I could until he pretended to ejaculate. All through the horrific episode I could see my friends peeping from the toilet. I got up and joined them in the bathroom while they both laughed asking me if I enjoyed it. I laughed and played along but deep down I felt very disgusted for even being in this situation and that I would forever share that secret with Yusef.

After we got dressed and joined Yusef back in the room, he pulled out 800 pounds from the stack he had initially promised us and walked out of the room. *What the hell?* I thought. I could see from the look on my friends' faces that we were thinking about the same thing. However, I knew why he changed his mind, and it was a secret I would carry to the grave. We split the money and called it a night. That was the last we heard of Yusef and I was relieved but the guilt from that night followed me.

When morning came, I decided to treat my girls to a day of

pampering courtesy of me. After all, they had worked for the money and with the guilt I felt the least I could do was spend it on them. We went for facials, manicure and pedicure. At the end of the spa day, we ended up at a restaurant somewhere on the island. It seemed pretty empty when we walked in but little did, we know there was an inner vip room with all the older men. We sat down and placed our food order. As we waited for our meal an older gentleman approached our table and asked us if we needed anything and if we could join his table in the inner room. Being nosey, we agreed. The inner room was a very cold dark room with blue lighting filled with men and younger girls sitting around.

We sat down with this man, and he introduced himself as Kayode. He told us he co-owned the restaurant and Tina's face lit up with excitement. She loved talking to only the bosses because it gave her bragging rights. He continuously offered us drinks and insisted we tell him if we wanted anything else. After we finished dining together, Kayode asked if we could exchange numbers and before I could get the word 'no' out Tina kicked me under the table. I immediately knew what that meant and told him yes instead. We had spent the day getting pampered and stuffing our faces for free.

Kayode called later in the day to check if we were home safe and after assuring him, he wished me a goodnight. The next afternoon he called us to come join him for lunch and we gladly went. In no time we were eating there at least 5 times a week for free. One thing led to another and Kayode asked me to be his girlfriend, or shall I say sugar baby and I thought what the hell. I was already getting free food and alcohol from him so why not add cash gifts. We were hanging out almost every day at the restaurant and one evening he asked if he could accompany me back home. I was reluctant at first but ended up agreeing to his request.

We got back to my guesthouse late in the evening. We continued talking and watching TV and out of the blue he made his move. He kissed me, but as repulsive as it was, I didn't stop him. Kayode had grown on me, and I didn't feel so bad kissing him. The kiss turned intense, and we eventually had sex, the first married man I slept with. After the sex he got dressed and left. I texted Tina immediately to invite her back to the room where I told her everything. Tina was happy, but even happier because I had locked in free food for as long as possible. I, on the other hand, was filled with disdain. I just slept with a man my father's age or older yuck! I was utterly disgusted with myself, and I couldn't stop picturing our shameful act.

One day I went to run errands and after a long day, I stopped to grab a quick bite and a couple cocktails in the hotel lobby of Oriental hotel, that was where I bumped into Ambassador T, an older gentleman. He was probably in his late thirties, married with kids and on the prowl. He sat down across from me on my table and offered to buy me a bottle of champagne. Since I was going to be there a bit longer because I was waiting for Tina and a couple other girls, I agreed. We started talking and he told me a little about himself, what he did for a living, and he made sure to let me know how rich he was. I didn't doubt it at all because it was written all over him. His arrogance popped out every so often.

My friends joined me later and when they got there, he rendered more drinks. It became a party, we laughed and drank till night time. It was too late to go home so he offered to get me a room in the hotel. I just guessed he wanted to be close to me, so I agreed. Tina and I spent the night in our room and by morning went back to the guest house to pack our things and settle into our new room. Later that evening ambassador T stopped by to visit.

I was still romantically involved with Kayode, and we saw each other from time to time. Ambassador T had become my boyfriend too, and he took care of all my hotel expenses, while Kayode handled food. Ambassador T had a best friend who was raw and uncouth, Lanre. He seemed a bit younger and not as rich as his friend. He picked a liking to Tina, and she equally liked him back. From day one he had been pressuring Tina to have sex with him, but she refused because he was yet to prove himself by giving her the money she demanded. They began an awkward yet toxic relationship but deep down I sensed he was only with Tina because he wanted to be close to me.

T and I had gotten much closer and spent a lot of time together. He was always playing the nice guy until one day Lanre invited us over to their penthouse suite. It was about 10pm and we thought we would be coming for drinks as we normally did. On getting to the room, we rang the doorbell and Lanre opened the door naked. Tina screamed as I stood there in shock *"Lanre what the hell, are you insane?"*. He laughed and pulled her into the room and as I walked in, Ambassador T was equally laying naked in a bed with two naked ladies on both sides of him. So much for the nice guy antics ugh! He saw me, and immediately jumped up in disbelief while I stood there and stared at him in utter disgust. Lanre was carefree and hoped we would join in on the fun as he aggressively tried to undress Tina, but received a slap instead. We left the room completely disgusted by their act. I was livid at the fact I wasted my time getting to know this man and the entire time he was a filthy scoundrel. He was no better than Ben, Yusef or any older man to be honest. It was then I realized it would always be about the sex for them.

T and Lanre had become a thing of the past and I decided to move on. Tina and I constantly gloated over not sleeping with any of them. One day we were buying pizza from dominos when we were approached by an Igbo man, Chief Mike. He looked fat, slightly sloppy and just plain ugly. He came over and said to me *"beautiful girl, what is your name"*

"Anna" I responded, and he continued with praises of how beautiful I was. While we were each waiting for our pizzas, he began showing his wealth off and eventually asked for my number. We exchanged contacts and said our goodbyes. You must be probably wondering why I gave him my number after calling him repulsive, the answer is I don't know. I had encountered so many men asking for my number that I began playing a game with myself. For every third guy that asked for my number I would have to give it to him even if he was the gateman, luckily, I had no gatemen asking for my numbers whew! Well Chief Mike happened to be the third man, whether I liked it or not I had to give him my number or lose my imaginary game and I hated losing.

After 3 days of talking on the phone he asked If I would have dinner with him and I honored his invitation. I invited two of my friends for dinner because I always felt safer with Tina around me, she had literally become my bodyguard. During dinner he asked for us to talk in private, so we walked outside and sat in the garden and that was where he told me he wanted to date me. In addition to that, he gave me an offer I couldn't refuse. *"You will be my girlfriend, and I will be sending you monthly allowance of 170,000k monthly, shopping trips and vacations anywhere in the world, you name it*" I had no choice but to accept, for a 22-year-old in 2013 that was a sweet deal, we sealed the deal with a kiss, a horrible one that almost had me gagging!

I couldn't wait to share the news with Tina. I knew she would be more excited than I was. At this point I had become the breadwinner in our little friendship, everything we spent came from the men I was juggling, and Tina became my bank accountant. I got home very excited and eager to tell her the good news but to my surprise, she was upset by the news. *"He looks like a ritualist, I don't trust him, and you shouldn't either"* she said. I laughed it off, but Tina remained unsettled. Chief Mike started coming to visit me and every time he came, he brought bundles of cash for me and because of that I didn't need the previous guys. I woke up one day and blocked all access the other guys had to me. Chief Mike became my full-time sugar daddy. After work he would stop by our hotel room to have dinner with us and even though Tina couldn't stand him, she had no choice but to tolerate his presence.

On this day, I got a phone call from Chief Mike telling me his driver would pick me up and bring me to his guest house in Dolphin estate Ikoyi. I had never been there before, and I was reluctant to meet him anywhere outside my hotel. Besides after Tina's constant nagging about him being a ritualist, I didn't feel safe. I tried to wiggle myself out of that agreement, but he insisted. I even tried to squeeze Tina into the plans, but he refused, the thought of him using me for rituals constantly poked at me. I put my big girl panties on and hopped in his car and followed his driver to the location. When I arrived, he had a room waiting for me and dinner prepared which I thought was cute, but I was still skeptical. We ended up drinking and he started kissing me. After the first kiss I knew where he was going with this and at this point, I was ready to run. I started making up excuses as to why I was not going to sleep with him, but it entered one ear and went out through the other, he didn't care if I wanted it or not, he was going to get it, and after a while of constantly pushing him off I gave in. I closed my eyes and willed it to be over quickly so I could go home.

After the sex I immediately stood up, rushed to the bathroom to take a quick shower. I couldn't wait to get his bodily fluids off me, I scrubbed myself hard in hopes that I would wash him off me. While in the shower tears began rolling down my eyes, I had finally reached my breaking point. Being sexually involved with all these men had taken a toll on me and sleeping with Chief Mike was the straw that broke the camel's back. I spent fifteen minutes in the shower crying my eyes out, filled with regret and disdain. As I dried myself off, Chief Mike walked in and told me he would be leaving and asked me to spend the night, which I agreed. I was in no shape to go back and face Tina, so I spent the night alone with nothing but my thoughts.

Few hours later, I heard a loud knock on the door, and I jumped out of bed, realizing I was still in his guesthouse, *"who is it? I asked"* as he replied saying *"it's me Mike"*. The flashbacks from the night before plagued my mind and I became sad all over again. I opened the door and Mike came in with breakfast and a dress and said *"I brought you breakfast and a change of clothes"* I thought to myself why the hell is he bringing me clothes, ugly clothes at that. I thanked him and proceeded to eat my breakfast as he informed me of the plans, he made for us to spend the entire day together and he wasn't letting me wiggle out of any of these plans. I spent the entire day following him around town, running errands, sitting in his office and when evening came, we went to meet up with his friends to have dinner. The entire day, I couldn't wait to get home and sleep, because I needed to clear my head. The guilt was wearing me down and every time he spoke or touched me, I felt nauseated. He made my skin crawl and gave me goosebumps but not in a good way.

I eventually went home and told Tina what I had been up to but left out the sex part because I wasn't ready to speak on it and to be honest, she wasn't ready to hear it. Over the next few weeks Chief Mike became overprotective, almost obsessive over me. He tried his hardest to alienate me from my friends, especially Tina who he didn't like. He would force me to sit in his office all day working with him, he even tried controlling the way I dressed. If I ever wore anything he thought was rather too revealing or he didn't like, he would drive me to a boutique nearby and pick something out by himself. I became exhausted. He was acting like my dad rather than a boyfriend, so I began plotting my escape from him. I started being rude and disrespectful towards him thinking it would stop him from seeing me but rather he became even more condescending and slightly aggressive towards me when he didn't get his way. To get my mind off the way things were going and the man I was sleeping next to every other night I began doing cocaine again, lots of it. It made me numb to everything going on around me and most importantly the sex to Chief Mike. Before he would come over, I would do a few lines every couple minutes just to keep me out of the loop and in no time, I became addicted to cocaine. It became my coping mechanism, my escape from reality and it felt damn good.

I continued to snort a couple lines of cocaine and down a couple patron shots every time I was going to see Chief Mike so I could live with myself and not feel the guilt and embarrassment. I became numb. Slowly my days became shorter and my nights longer. I was living in a hotel and having sex with a man who I despised so much. Seeing him walk into my room whenever he felt like and demanding for sex had me depressed. I could no longer tolerate it and one day I packed up all my belongings and Tina's and we ditched the hotel

Chief Mike lodged us in and I blocked his number. Now we were homeless and needed somewhere to stay.

Tina had started seeing an older man who she was spending her days and nights with, Niyi. He owned a beautiful house in Victoria Island and an expensive garage. He was filthy rich but stingy as ever, at least to Tina he was. She convinced him to let us spend a couple days at his place until we figured out a plan and he agreed. First night there, we had dinner and Niyi opened a bottle of champagne while he familiarized himself with me. By the end of the night, I said my goodbyes and hurried on to the guestroom to sleep. It had been a long day and I was coming down from a cocaine high, so my mood had been fluctuating all day. I just needed to sleep it off and due to how beautiful his house was I felt safe and at home.

I was getting undressed and ready for bed when Niyi barged in, *"your friend is calling you in the other room"* he said with a slimy look on his face. All through the night Niyi had given me perverted vibes. He constantly licked his lips while staring at my breast or butt and made sexual comments all night. To be honest it bothered me at first, but Tina assured me it was just the way he was and as long as she was comfortable with it, I couldn't complain.

I walked into his master bedroom, and saw Tina laying in his bed with a certain sadness in her eyes, *"what's wrong, is everything okay?"* I asked as I sat beside her, she says to me *"I know you're going to think I'm crazy but just listen to me please, Niyi wants to have sex with you right now and he's willing to give you $3,000 this night"*

What? I yelled as I stood up from the bed, *how can you say that, isn't he your man?*

"To be honest, I don't care, its money and we need it so why the hell not"

I knew Tina like the palm of my hand, she did care. As a matter of fact, she was probably heartbroken, once again a Nigerian man had proven himself to be untrusty and driven by sex. I blatantly refused, not only did I feel like I was betraying a friend but the thought of getting paid to have sex with this man had me in distress. You might be thinking well it is not different from what you were doing with the others? To an extent that might be true, but with the others there was a preexisting relationship, some form of commitment, even though I hated it all the same it felt way better than what I was about to get myself into.

Niyi walked into the room thinking everything had been handled but to his surprise I politely turned down his advances and walked to my room. A couple minutes later Tina and Niya barged in and this time

Niyi had an even bigger offer- $5,000. Now this was an offer Tina wasn't letting up on. At this point she wanted that money more than she wanted her relationship with Niyi because she had come to the realization that Niyi wasn't a stingy man, he just never saw her fit to spend his money on. After her constant pleading and nagging I agreed to have sex with her boyfriend and before we began, I made sure to run into the bathroom, snort a couple lines and stall till it kicked in.

I laid in the bed staring at the ceiling while Niyi climbed on top of me and had his way. Once he finished, he kissed me on the forehead and went back to his room to join Tina while I cleaned myself up with tears in my eyes. By morning, I was ready to go and put the night behind me. Niyi handed me an envelope containing dollars, he whispered to me to come back alone, and he would pay me double, I smiled, collected my money and walked out of the door filled with contempt. We arrived at our new hotel room, unpacked, got settled and took a long nap. When I woke up, I saw Tina from the corner of my eye exchanging text messages with Niyi and from the way she was typing I could tell they were arguing over something. I knew deep down she was hurt by his actions but her love for money was more than anything he could have done to her, and I always wondered how she really felt towards me after that night. Oh well I guess we would never know.

We hit the streets that night in celebration of our new funds, and we ended up in a club in Victoria Island. We made our way to the bar and ordered our first round of drinks when we were approached by a gentleman who asked us to buy him a drink. Tina, being her rude self, instantly shut him down and asked him to leave but I, on the other hand, offered him a drink. He accepted my offer and thanked me for my kindness, it turns out his name was Mohamed and he was the owner of the club. We spent the night dancing and drinking champagne on his table, by the end of the night we exchanged numbers.

Two days later Tina and I were invited to his house for dinner. It was a nice setting and he made us very comfortable. His chef cooked and served us a lovely dinner. After eating he decided to give us a tour of his house and asked that we talk in private. He began telling me how much he liked me from the first day he set his eyes on me and how he wanted to date me. I was not in any relationship at that time, and I didn't see any harm in being in one, so I agreed to be in a relationship with him.

A couple months into the relationship, Mohamed and I became very close, and I spent most of my nights at his house with Tina, where she occupied one of his guest rooms. While dating him I was only allowed to party at his club and sit at his table. He was a sweet guy but very controlling and jealous. I became his lover and travel companion; I went with him on trips all over the world. He was the first man I got to travel with, and we flew everywhere together from Paris to Las Vegas, to New York and Miami. I got to shop as much as I wanted and ordered all the room service I wanted.

Even with all the luxury I was enjoying with Mohamed, I was still not attracted to him. I was solely in it for the perks and no matter how much I shopped and ate, the feeling of emptiness remained. At this time, I couldn't function without drugs, I couldn't stand to face my reality, I couldn't handle not being sober so I stayed drugged up as much as I could. Once again, I reached a peak, a peak I could no longer live with, so I walked out of Mohamed's life without an explanation. He was devastated, he had grown to love me, and oftentimes he would talk to me about his long-term goals which included us getting married and relocating to another country. I knew it would never happen because I would have never let it. After my relationship with Mohamed, I decided I wanted to go back to dating regular guys my age again and maybe it would fill the void, so I became more receptive to younger men.

Chapter 11

Yahoo boys!

A Yahoo boy, or G boy, he is a fraudster in short, popularly known for either scamming or hacking into bank accounts, and amassing wealth by stealing from unsuspecting individuals, through illegal means.

Tina and I started partying a lot more. We were in the club almost every night of the week, drinking alcohol and doing cocaine in the bathroom. Most nights we were so drunk that we wouldn't remember how we made it home. Our days were spent sleeping while we partied all night. Most of the guys in the club that were my age mates were either celebrities or yahoo boys[1].

It's almost impossible to not spot a yahoo boy in the club. He is always the flashiest in the crowd, always wearing new season designer clothes and always has an exaggerated amount of alcohol on his table. They always use aliases to hide their identity, you might hear random names like P-money, JoJo dollar or Femi boss, hilarious won't you agree?

Even though I had experienced dating yahoo boys in the states the guys in Lagos were a different ball game, they knew exactly what it took to keep a girl like me entertained, money! Every yahoo boy I encountered in Lagos was willing to spend heavily on me and cater to my every need and desire. There was something about me that had them so intrigued. Maybe it was because I was young, wild and free or the fact I loved to party, or my American citizenship, whatever it was, I was using it to my advantage, and I made them work for it. I had them chasing me all over the city.

On this particular day I received a snapchat message from a guy I had never met before telling me that he would love to hook me up with his boss. I thought that was weird as no one had ever reached out to me like that. We began chatting about his boss, and he told me his name was Prince and he was filthy rich and willing to spend a ton on me. Because of how awkward this conversation was I figured this mysterious person wanted something in return. As we chatted, I constantly waited to read *"and my cut is?"* but it never came. He only insisted I meet up with his boss and give him a chance. I agreed.

His boss followed me on snapchat moments later and said hi. I responded to his pleasantries. He went on to ask me a couple questions about myself and asked if we could meet up for drinks. Unfortunately, I wasn't too confident meeting up with a faceless person off a social media app, so I agreed to meet him but never showed up. After several failed meet up attempts, I finally decided to meet up with him and his friends in the club.

When I got to his table at the club, he stretched out his hand and whispered his name into my ear. At first glance he was not my choice, I was in no way attracted to this man even as a friend. From that moment, I knew whatever it is that we have would be short-lived and once I could finesse all I needed from him, his chapter would be history.

We partied a couple nights in a row, and he always made sure to drop my friends and I off at my hotel. One particular night, after we arrived at my hotel and my friends jumped out of the car I stayed behind a little longer. I had a plan to throw my first bill at him to see how much he thought I was worth. I asked him to pay to have my room extended and it would only cost N300,000. He laughed and asked for my account number and sent me one million naira instantly. I was shocked. He was an easy target, probably the easiest I had met, and I was ready to milk him dry.

I thanked him with a hug and said my goodbyes. A day later I was on a flight back to Houston. Months passed, and we kept in contact, I had grown on him, and he called and texted me almost every day. He started professing his love for me and how he was obsessed with me. He was a married man so there was nothing I could possibly want from him except money and all he wanted from me was sex. My plan was to get as much as I could before anything sexual would ever occur.

I decided to return to Nigeria for the holidays, so I informed him. He agreed to not only pay for my flight but also to book and pay for my accommodation. When I got into the country, he had his security detail pick me up and take me to my hotel, while he waited for me to eat and freshen up so we could go out to party. We went club hopping and eventually ended up at a Chinese restaurant where he decided to pour out his feelings for me. I was still unable to reciprocate the feeling, so I constantly shut him down and insisted on us taking things slow, but he kept assuring me, he wasn't just after sex.

We started dating after a few months. He constantly confided in me about his marriage and past relationships and told me stories about his wife and why he was miserable in his marriage. He kept insinuating he wanted to marry me, but because of my lack of feelings for him I constantly gave him marriage advice and tips to boost his marriage. I knew I had no feelings for him, so it was in my best interest to ensure his marriage worked. With each growing day Prince professed his undying love for me and all he wanted in return was my affection but sadly, I couldn't give it to him. Instead, I continued to emotionally blackmail him into thinking our relationship would have a happy ending while he catered to my every need.

He constantly loaded my bank account in an effort to impress me and to be honest I was impressed. I was yet to meet a man like Prince who was willing to give me the world without demanding for sex in return. After living in hotels for almost a year I decided I was ready to fully commit to Lagos and get my first apartment. And with Prince by my side paying for everything the process was easy, and in no time, I had moved into my first two-bedroom apartment in Lekki. In less than two months I had completely furnished my home to my taste.

I was able to acquire everything I wanted; I employed a maid, a chef and my very own driver. I was living what I thought was my dream - the Lekki big girl life. I loved my apartment, but something was missing, but I couldn't place my finger on it. *What could it have been, what was it that kept me up at night in deep thought?* One day, I figured it out - It was a car, but not just any car. *I needed something to fit my new island baddie lifestyle but how was I going to acquire this car?*

After months and months of pleading and persuading, I was finally able to convince Prince to buy me a Mercedes Benz C class. This car was all kinds of sexy and I couldn't wait to cruise down the streets of

Lekki in it. With this new ride came a new level of confidence, I felt untouchable, unstoppable and unbreakable. Nobody could tell me anything, I was on top of the world.

My girls and I would dress up and hit the clubs every night and the best part was, I had unlimited tabs in every nightclub I walked into. I never had to pay a dime for what I ordered, and Prince had a drug dealer who delivered drugs to me on request. *What more could a girl have asked for?* Unfortunately, with all that attention came drama and pettiness, people I called friends started becoming jealous of me. There were rumors about me and I constantly found my name being brought up in gatherings I knew nothing about. It became so bad that whenever I met someone casually and I mentioned my name the first thing I got in response would be *"oh you're the Amanda I'm constantly hearing about?"*

I was attracting all the wrong attention and to be honest that was not what I wanted, I wanted to be the girl silently cashing out yet living her best life, but when you're living in Lagos and running with the wrong set of people, drama is inevitable. I took a step back to reevaluate my life and my surroundings. Although I had done quite well for my age, there was a void that needed to be filled and no matter how much alcohol and drugs I took it refused to go away. Some nights I would be filled with so much love and energy while other nights I was filled with regret and sorrow, even in a room full of people I could feel myself drowning. No matter how I tried to fill this void it only got deeper causing me to venture into more drugs and alcohol.

As my days grew longer and my nights shorter, I had started missing my old life in Houston- a life of structure and innocence, waking up to one man and going to sleep besides the same man. In Lagos it seemed almost impossible to find the right man, to find love, everyone was either chasing money or status. One of my exes once told me *"if you wanted to find true love you would have to give up certain things in life like money and luxury, because you can't eat your cake and have It"* and slowly, I was coming to that realization.

Chapter 12

Manju

All the while I was running the streets of Lagos, my heart truly belonged to one man - Peju Adewusi. He was one of the hottest nightclub promoters in town and you were guaranteed a great time at any of his events. From the first moment I saw him, I felt some kind of chemistry towards him. It was back in 2014, we met at once of the clubs he was promoting at the time. From his dressing to the way he danced, he reeked of confidence and arrogance at the same time. I needed a reason to get closer to him and luckily for me my friends at the time were familiar with his friends so getting through to him seemed easy.

I found every means to talk to him and finally I succeeded. The first day he spoke to me he said, *"you're the only girl in Lagos that parties every day and your hair doesn't smell like cigarettes and booze, what's your secret?"* I blushed and responded with a *"thank you"*. That day, I sensed he felt the same chemistry I felt. We constantly flirted with each other while I was in the states. It was more than just the usual fun for me, it was more like there was something about this guy I couldn't resist. The way I felt towards him was different from the other guys I had been with in the past.

At the time I met him, I was still fully in the street, and running the streets with different guys in Houston to even pay him any mind. One day he asked me a question and since then he always stood out in my mind. He said, *"when do you see yourself settling down, and how many kids do you want?"*. No man had ever asked me that before. It felt like he saw beyond just my body, he saw through my soul. I thought to myself *"this man is different from the rest"*

It was Christmas time and Peju said he wanted me around him, so he bought me a ticket to Lagos. When I got to Lagos, things became more serious, and we started a relationship. This was not a very serious relationship because we both had other people, we were seeing but being together felt magical, peaceful, and safe. Peju was living a very fast life, partying every night, traveling the world and shopping nonstop. Whispers round Lagos claims that he was into fraud which was believable at the time because he checked off all the boxes. To be honest I didn't mind, I was coming from a life of fraud and fraudsters so dating another one in Lagos didn't bother me at all. We barely talked when we were together, and I thought that was cute because we were both extremely shy around each other. However, no matter how awkwardly silent it was, it still felt good being in each other's presence.

Peju was a playboy, and that was due to the nature of his job. He partied every day and got laid every night. I, on the other hand, was heavy in the runz game but once our eyes locked nothing or no one else mattered. There were nights I was offered thousands of dollars to follow men home from the club which I would agree to, but the moment Peju walked in no one would be able to take me away from him. I was leaving the club with him and only him. My love for him grew each day and it began to piss Tina off because I was ruining our chances of making money.

Due to circumstances that surrounded us, his friends hated me, and my friends didn't like him either because I spent so much time with him. Peju and I fought a lot, one week we were all loved up and locking lips in the club, the next week we were walking past each other with dirty looks, but in all of that we were obsessed with each other. We couldn't resist staring at each other all night to the point of constantly trying to make the other person jealous. Our relationship was a roller coaster of emotions for years and in the summer of 2017, something happened that changed the course of our relationship.

Peju broke his ankle playing soccer and he had to wear a cast for some weeks. He called me and told me about it. Although he insisted, he was okay and could take care of himself, I cancelled my flight to the US so I could be with him. We were stuck in the house for weeks and during this time, I finally got to meet the real Peju

Adewusi. Due to his condition, he was in a very vulnerable position, and I got to witness him in his true nature without his arrogance or cockiness. He was like an overgrown baby, and I felt special knowing he chose to let me see him like that. Our bond grew stronger, and I started imagining myself giving up the game and becoming his wife, but I still had my doubts.

By the end of summer Peju's cast was taken off and he was able to move around again. Even though he still walked with a limp he was independent, so he didn't need me anymore. I decided to head back to the US and we spent the entire night kissing, cuddling and having sex. When it was morning, I headed to the airport. From the moment I kissed him goodbye, I knew I was going to miss him so much.

On my way to the airport, an idea came to me. Now that I am heading back to the US, I needed to be sure this man was worth leaving the game for so I came up with a plan to test him in hopes he wouldn't let me down. I called him immediately and told him my period was late.

Babe what do you mean your period was late, he asked

I mean I am pregnant babe

For real? He said in an exciting tone

Yes

So you mean I am going to be a father,

Yes babe

What's the plan? What do you think we should do?

Errrrrm, let me think about it and get back to you. I'm about to board, I'll call you when I land. Bye babe.

Although I was hoping he was going to be excited, I was very surprised at his reaction. He sounded so excited that I started to feel bad that I lied. I wished it was true. I called at the spur of the moment and didn't think this through, now I have to come up with a plan. But what I realized at that point was, he was totally worth it.

As I landed in Houston and settled in, Peju and I began planning our life with a baby; a baby I wasn't carrying. I had told a bold face lie and now I was stuck in my lie. I figured the only way to get out of this lie was to insist that I get an abortion. Unfortunately for me, Peju wanted this child. I also wanted the same because I was head over heels for this man, but the problem was, I wasn't pregnant. We argued for weeks about my decision to get an abortion, he was not letting down no matter how hard I tried. He had a solution for every excuse I came up with. I became sick, tired and overly sensitive. This was looking beyond emotional stress so I decided to take a pregnancy test. Lo and behold the test read positive in all capital letters. Now I was really screwed. I already told him I was carrying his child for weeks prior to finding out and even though I wanted to keep this pregnancy the lies made it almost impossible. There was no way I could explain the discrepancies. My stupid game had put me in a compromising situation and without a doubt I went through with an abortion.

Peju was dealing with his own personal issues, from breaking his ankle to some run-ins with the law. Few weeks after my abortion, he told me he gave his life to Christ. I was quite surprised but happy for him. After then, he became so distant and eventually broke things off with me. I was heartbroken and filled with regret. I gave so much of myself to this man, and he just threw it all away so easily. He didn't even have the decency to break up with me properly, all he did was send a lousy text message. That made the hurt even worse. I tried to understand why, but every time I asked, he insisted I had to be born again for the relationship to prosper. At that time, I didn't even know what going to church meant, let alone giving my life to Christ. I was far from walking that path with him and even though I tried to forcefully change my ways and habits, deep down I knew I was only lying to myself and Peju knew it too.

Two months later I returned to Lagos and continued where I had left off- partying, drinking and drugs. I got in contact with Prince and he was back at my beck and call like before. Our relationship was waxing strong but through it all I knew my heart belonged to Peju and nothing was going to stop me from being with him. I knew being with him was a long shot, but I never lost hope. Although Peju was born again he still worked as a club promoter, crazy right? *How can someone become born again and yet be in the club almost every night?* Well luckily for me those were the only days I got to sneak peeks at him, hoping he would somehow fall in love with me again.

After months of ignoring me, he walked over to me one night and started a conversation. One thing led to another, and I convinced him to follow me back to my hotel room so we could talk. To my surprise, he agreed. We talked for a long time and when he realized it was too late, he decided to spend the night with me. We slept side by side and didn't even think of touching each other. Late into the night, I heard a voice outside my room door and thought nothing of it so I went back to sleep. A couple seconds later, Prince barged into the room, walked up to the bed, stood there watching us as we laid there in a state of shock, murmured something under his breath and stormed out of my room. "*Somebody wake me up from this horrible nightmare*" I thought to myself as I slowly turned to look at Peju. I could see the disappointment written all over his face. "*wow Amanda, you really fucked up this time,*" I thought. Peju refused to say a word but from the look on his face I knew that this night would be the last night I would probably ever see him again.

***

After my mother died, I lost hope in marriage. I shied away from the thought of getting married because my mother wouldn't be there to witness it. *Who would walk me down the aisle?* Yes, I have a father who's very much alive, but our relationship is almost nonexistent. *How am I supposed to share that day with him?*

Half of my life I hid the truth about my mother from my exes. Most of them believed she was still alive living in New York. I never understood why I hid the truth from them, I guess I never really wanted to share my emotions or have anyone feel sorry for me. Whenever marriage conversations came up, I would quickly change the topic or make a joke and laugh my way out of it. I was emotionally distant. Anytime I sensed a serious commitment I would slowly begin to sabotage that relationship and over time I became scared of long-lasting commitments. Even though I was in a couple of long-term relationships, deep down I knew I was just in them for fun and companionship and because I hated sleeping alone.

A year went by, and it seemed as if every time I bumped into Peju his hatred for me grew more. *How was I ever supposed to make amends for that night if he can't even stand to be in the same room with me?* but I never gave up. I was determined to make amends. All my friends thought I was crazy for even thinking I had a chance with him after that night. I knew what I was praying for and eventually my prayers were answered.

Two years after our fallout Peju eventually walked up to me in the club on one of his drunken nights and whispered something in my ear. I was equally as drunk, so I didn't understand what he said but I thought that was the perfect opportunity to make my move since he was in a forgiving mood. "*I miss you*", I said. He looked at me and smiled. My heart skipped a bit when he responded with "I *miss you too*". That moment I knew I was never letting go again. I was sure this was my last bus stop - my husband.

Over the next few months, we spent every waking day beside each other. It was almost like we were making up for lost time. We both had our separate apartments, but I had almost fully moved into his, abandoning mine. At the end of our leases, we decided to get a place together. Our relationship was going great, and everyone seemed to be obsessed with our union. We became a celebrity couple overnight. We even had a cocktail named after us "MANJU ". During this time, we moved into our first home and began our journey to commitment.

Our relationship quickly became the talk of time and in no time, we were the topic of conversation in every social group. We started getting offers for television shows, endorsements, and event hosting. We were "THE COUPLE" and most people envied us while others imagined what our relationship was like behind closed doors. To be honest it was perfect, I was dating the man I prayed for. I didn't have to hide my past because he knew me - the real me and I knew him too. We were a match made in heaven. Unfortunately, there are consequences for reckless behavior.

Since we got back together, we decided to have a baby. We were trying actively to have a baby and did everything we could. All we did was party and have fun, but we thought we were ready to become parents. December 2018, I found out I was pregnant. I was filled with excitement and planned a special way to tell Peju. I wrapped the pregnancy test in a gift box and left it on his pillow. He stumbled on the box while he was preparing to sleep. He tore it up and screamed in excitement when he saw the box. *"Oh my God, Babe you're pregnant?"* he asked. I smiled and nodded my head. I watched his face lit with excitement as he hugged me tightly and began kissing my stomach.

I immediately quit alcohol and drugs and began trying to live a healthier lifestyle. One day, Peju and I went to an event we were invited to. After the event, we decided to enter the club. I was feeling cramps all day and thought nothing of it, but I noticed with each passing hour the pain grew stronger. I chose to brush it off so as to not ruin the fun night we were having. At around 1am, the pain had become unbearable, and I could no longer tolerate it. I told Peju I needed to go to the restroom, he accompanied me and waited for me outside and I made my way inside.

After urinating, I wiped myself and saw traces of blood on the tissue. I thought nothing of it. When I turned to flush the toilet, I saw something dark inside the toilet, still I thought nothing of it *"maybe it was in there before I peed"* I thought to myself. I flushed, came out, washed my hands and joined Peju outside. At this point, I started feeling dizzy and was sweating profusely, so we decided to rush home. As I was walking up the staircase to our bedroom, blood was rushing down my legs. The pain got so bad, I started to cry. I could no longer walk upstairs, so I sat down on the staircase until Peju eventually carried me up and into the bed. Little did I know I had a miscarriage.

We decided we needed an escape from everything we had been going through. It felt like our world had slowly come crashing down around us and we had no one to confide in but ourselves. We spent the next couple months traveling in search of solitude. Peju's birthday was approaching so I decided it was the perfect time for us to take a trip to another country. I booked a trip to Mahe Seychelles - a beautiful island located in the Indian ocean in an east African country. It was a surprise birthday getaway where we could relax and strategize our lives. Seychelles was beautiful, we had never seen a place so beautiful and we got to experience it as a couple.

While in Seychelles we met a man, a wealthy man who seemed intrigued by our appearance. He introduced himself to us as John. John came off rather strong and we assumed he wanted to sleep with me or somehow become extra friendly with me. He offered to pick us up and take us to dinner that same day. It was weird that an older man we were just meeting for the first time was pausing his life to entertain us. It seemed odd, and we were sure there must be a catch so we patiently waited all night for it. To our surprise there wasn't, he was just a man that liked us and saw something in us and instantly we created a bond.

The next day John picked us up again and took us all around town. Our first stop was his office where he had lunch waiting for us and immediately served us when we arrived. I must say it was the best thing we ate while on the island. After that he took us to his house- a mansion right in the heart of the island. It was the most beautiful house I had ever seen with a stunning ocean view and a private beach in his backyard. We were blown away but still couldn't figure why this man had become so personal with us. Coming from a country where most men his age only wanted one thing- sex, it was hard to trust John.

No matter how nice and accommodating John was, I constantly waited for him to make his move. I always kept an eye on him because it was hard for me to believe he was just being genuine. Till the day we left, he didn't spring any surprises, that was when we realized he was just an honest man trying to make our trip worthwhile.

Coming back home to Lagos, I was filled with bitter emotions, and we started to feel sad almost instantly. Things started going wrong right from the airport. It was like the country was pre designed to frustrate us so we began researching other countries we could go to. After a week we decided we would take another trip to Sierra Leone. Something about that country seemed like the perfect place to continue our tour. Once again, we booked a trip, but this time, a friend of ours who is a celebrity helped us get a sponsor which means the trip was free. When we got to Sierra Leone, we met an influential

Nigerian man who once again took a liking to us and immediately introduced himself, and a friendship began. We eventually met the Nigerian ambassador to Sierra Leone and a couple other influential people while touring the country. It was a moment of rest for us, and we got to put all the stress of the previous months behind.

Chapter 13

Jezebel!

A couple months after returning from Sierra Leone, I discovered I was pregnant again. We spent the entire year cleaning up our act. We limited the way we partied, cut off some friends, started eating healthier and started making better choices. We were so happy to have been given another chance, so we decided to give this baby a fighting chance and leave the rest to God. Every day we lived in fear of once again losing our baby. April 2nd, 2020, Legend Adewusi was born, my beautiful baby boy. He came into our lives and changed it for the better. He showed us the true meaning of God's love and gave us a whole new purpose for life.

After my mother died, I felt life had been unfair to me. I watched my mother constantly pray for God to heal her. We weren't a strong Christian family; we barely even went to church on Sundays, but I watched her become best friends with her bible during her illness. I was too young to understand why, so when she died, I became furious with everything and everyone, most especially God. I felt He could have spared her life; he could have given her more time on earth, but he took her away from us and left us stranded and confused. I began to question my existence and the more I questioned it the angrier I became. I developed a hatred for anything that had to do with church or God, I disliked pastors and the idea of worship.

It's safe to say I became an atheist without even knowing. I was living life angry. Every time I heard someone pray or mention the name of God I would be consumed with rage, an inexplicable rage almost like something had taken over me. So many times, I attempted suicide and yet I wouldn't die. I manifested an evil inside of me that began to speak to me and try to convince me to do vile things. For many years I was possessed by the jezebel spirit.

Jezebel! For those of you who have never heard of her, she was described in the bible as a princess, daughter to a Phoenician king Ethbaal (1 kings 16:31). She got married to Ahab, king of Israel. She was known as a woman who embodied wickedness, and evil. She used her position and influence on her husband the king to lie, steal, murder and persecute the prophets of God (1 kings 21:5-16). She convinced Ahab to abandon the worship of God and join her in promoting the worship of idols- Baal and Asherah, eventually causing the people of Israel to reject God, and destroy the altars dedicated to the worship of God

For many years I battled with the spirit of Jezebel (a demonic spirit that inhabits a person and causes them to be driven by sexual appetites.) I felt as if my purpose on earth was to seduce and destroy men. Most of my childhood was plagued with vivid nightmares of a woman either trying to strangle me or choke me as I slept. These nightmares followed me into adulthood and made me scared of sleeping. I was scared of what the woman would do every night. I was scared of not waking up from the nightmare. I spent many nights fighting my sleep until I could no longer hold off. And the moment I fell asleep, she would strike again.

I remember one of the scenarios vividly. In this particular dream, I was in the backseat of a car while a woman was driving through what seemed like a forest. It was daytime so it felt normal. Suddenly, we stopped, and a bunch of men surrounded the car and started trying to force their way into the car. The windows were slightly down so they put their hands and grabbed me out of the car. The moment I was out of the car, they started pulling me in different directions in an attempt to strip my clothes off. The entire time I was looking at this woman begging her for help, but she kept staring at me and didn't help. This torture went on until I woke up in a pool of sweat.

Most times I would wake up screaming, scaring my friends. I remember the night terrors like it was yesterday. The thought of it still freaks me out. One time I woke up to find a woman sitting at the edge of my bed wearing dark sunglasses. Looking at her the first time, I assumed it was my mother but as I attempted to speak, she began pinching my right foot. It was so painful that I can remember the feeling as I type this.

Most of my adult life was spent in a state of confusion, confusion with my purpose, confusion in my relationships. I hated men but I still got into serious relationships with them but the moment I sensed a serious commitment coming on I would find a reason to terminate it. I dabbled in lesbianism at a young age because I felt safer with women. I thought I could find what I wanted in a man in a woman. Because of everything I had experienced with men in the past I thought I could find peace and solace in women while I get the material things from men.

In the search of protecting myself from men, I was introduced to jazz by my cab driver at the time. He came to pick me up one day from the house of a well-known politician and began advising me to move with caution as most of them are well known for dabbling with the occultic. He insisted that I followed him to a baba, a voodoo doctor. I refused blatantly because that was something I knew I couldn't see myself doing but he assured me that all I needed to do was give him money and the rest would be handled.

We drove forty minutes to the other side of town, a very local settlement just outside of Lagos where this baba lived. He was well known for doing charms for good luck, favor and protection from evil. As he approached the car my heart began to beat fast. I was consumed with fear of my surroundings and what would happen next. Baba couldn't speak English, so he greeted us in a Yoruba dialect and began asking us questions. My cab driver began to converse with him in their language explaining what it was that we had come for. Although I trusted my cab driver, a small part of me wondered if he was a bad person.

Baba walked back into his house as we sat outside waiting and after some time he returned and sat inside the car with us. He pulled out a little black bag and emptied the contents on the chair, revealing an item wrapped in red cloth. He proceeded to explain to my cab Guy what it was and how I was meant to use it, while my cab guy translated it to me. Before seeing any man, I was meant to lift the item to my tongue and speak my demands into it and the person's name who I was seeking it from, then wrap it back up and hide it away. Nobody was meant to set their eyes on it aside from me or touch it. After demonstrating how it would be used, he wrapped it up, spoke some incantations over it and placed it in the palm of my hand alongside another little pouch which contained what looked to be black powder. I was meant to pour a little of the powder under my tongue before going out; he said it acted as my protection.

On getting back to Lagos, I noticed how excited my cab driver was so I asked him his reason for the excitement, and he said, *"now you will be very rich and powerful, and I will become your personal driver"*. I laughed and thought *"wow all of this just to become my personal driver, deep"*. Every night as I was preparing to head out into the streets, I would pull out my jazz, and speak my affirmations into it and in no time, I had become attached to it.

I believed so much in this jazz that I carried it everywhere with me until one day I was stopped by TSA airport security on one of my trips back to the US. I was asked to follow them to the back office where they thoroughly searched my bags and brought them out. I guess the powdered substance had triggered an alert. I watched as they carefully unwrapped my jazz and I started to panic because I remembered the instructions from the baba that no one was allowed to see it or touch it. The fear of something happening to me consumed my mind as I waited for the airport security to take the items to the back and test them. He eventually brought them back and asked what they were and the reason I had them. I told him they were African ornaments, and he handed them back to me and gave me the permission to pack my things and leave. *Whew! that was close,* I thought to myself as I walked out of the airport. I tossed them into the trash and that was the end of that chapter.

I cried myself to sleep on so many days. On the outside, it seemed like I was living the life most girls envied, but on the inside, I was unhappy, severely depressed, and curing my sadness with alcohol and hard drugs. So many times, I would go for P and after having sex with these men I would break down in tears while I was still in bed. I never knew what was wrong with me, but I knew I needed saving, I needed healing. Once I got back together with Peju, I vowed to put the P life behind me and commit to him and only him, and our relationship has been going great.

When I got back to Nigeria in December 2020, we set up a date to tie the knot, Ja*nuary 15th, 2021.* The stress of being a new mom had taken a toll on me and before I knew it, I slipped back into a slight depression and started using drugs again. As our wedding date approached, so did my anxiety and I started acting out of character. Things I enjoyed no longer interested me. All I wanted to do was stay in bed all day long and do drugs the moment Peju stepped out of the house.

Two weeks after our wedding I received a phone call from a guy I used to go out with. He reached out asking me to come visit him. He said he had a gift for me and wanted us to meet up at his house. I told Peju and out of the trust he had for me he gave me the permission to go ahead. When I got there, he offered me champagne, we caught up on old times and did drugs. One thing led to another we had sex and he gave me a large sum of cash in return as I prepared to head back home. The car ride home seemed like the longest ride ever. I was filled with the feelings of guilt and regret *"how could I go so long being faithful and finally decide to cheat two weeks after getting married, am I possessed?"* I had absolutely no explanation as to why I had just done what I did. A part of me seemed to have craved my past of carelessly sleeping around, partying and doing drugs, while the other half regretted. That night's event was a secret I was willing to carry to the grave. I continued living my life as if nothing had ever happened that night and the following week I was back in the US.

As I returned to my normal life in the US and tried to put the entire December behind me. I started noticing some strange changes in my system. Over the next couple of months, my menstrual cycle became very painful and unbearable. My flow was heavier and lasted longer than usual. At first, I thought nothing of it because I thought my body was still adapting to motherhood. After 4 consistent months of experiencing this pain, I had to confide in Peju. He advised me to pray over the issue and seek God's deliverance.

One day as I watched a sermon on TV, a strong feeling came over me and I decided to give my life to Christ. I knelt and prayed for God's forgiveness and started a spiritual fast. During my fast, God began to reveal himself to me in a series of dreams, but I didn't understand these dreams at the time. One morning I woke up, I knelt and prayed for direction and that God should reveal my purpose in life, and how I needed to live my life for his honor. Almost instantly I began to hear a loud voice in my head asking me to confess to Peju about what happened, I refused, and ignored the voice but for some reason it got louder and louder. I tried distracting myself, maybe if I washed the dishes, watched a movie or talked on the phone I would shake this voice out of my head. I was wrong, no matter what I did the voice followed me around and only got louder as I ignored it.

I swallowed my pride and called Peju and broke the news to him. To my surprise he wasn't as angry as I expected. He claimed the thought came across his mind that night because of how I was acting when I returned home. We talked about it and prayed about it. He forgave me almost instantly, and the burden I had been carrying for months finally eased up. I felt lighter than I had ever felt before. I continued my fasting and prayer and one night I had the weirdest dream ever. In this dream, I was visited by family members and as we all sat eating dinner and catching up on old times, my cousin looked up at me as if she had been possessed and immediately started yelling *"whatever you are experiencing is the result of what you did, you cheated on Peju and on Tuesday you will find out what is inside of you, what the man you slept with put inside of you while pointing to my stomach"*. In this dream, I was filled with shame as everyone sat down judging me. I began to explain to them that I wasn't pregnant, and it wasn't what they thought, but the secret had been let out and everyone was looking up at me in disappointment, that was when I woke up.

I couldn't shake off the dream from my head. I kept trying to put the pieces together but what stood out the most to me was the date mentioned in my dream. I quickly turned over, grabbed my phone, pulled up my calendar and noticed that the Tuesday 10th of august had been marked on my calendar. I realized a doctor's appointment had been set for that date. I jumped out of bed in a panic, my dream started to make some sense. Whatever it was that this man had put inside of me would be revealed on that date at my doctor's appointment, which was booked two months in advance. I knelt and began to praise God for he had once again revealed something so great to me.

Two weeks after my dream I went for my doctor's appointment where he revealed to me, I had endometrial polyps (mostly common in women who are undergoing or have completed menopause). He scheduled me for immediate surgery the following week. The surgery was successful. After the surgery, I felt a relief I had longed for months. The torture was finally over, God had spared me once again.

As the days went by, I began reading my bible and the story of jezebel caught my attention. I picked a peculiar interest in her story, because something about her seemed familiar. One night I prayed to God to reveal to me if I was being possessed or haunted by the spirit of jezebel and help me fight it. God revealed what I suspected, as

One night in my dream, I saw a woman standing outside my window, she wore something that looked like a royal regalia. She danced outside my window and as I watched her in fear it seemed as if she was trying to lure me to let her back in. I continued to watch in fear, not heading to her advances. She became furious and began slamming on the door demanding to be let back in, that was when I woke up and realized jezebel no longer had a resting place in my body, I was free from her control.

Since I gave my life to Christ, I have found peace, a peace I had not known for 29 years of my existence. I finally have direction and purpose in my life, and I know I am on a path to something bigger than I ever imagined. This new phase of my life is predisposed to change and making sure I do not fall back into the hole I once found myself in. I am on a journey of self, turning a new leaf and becoming the best version of myself, the version God wants me to be. Nobody knows what the future may hold but I am living in the now and trusting in the process. God has been merciful to me over the years, and this is how I will show my commitment to him.

To God be the Glory!

"It is not true that everyone is special. It is true that everyone was once special and still possesses the ability to recover it,"

- Criss Jami, 'Killosophy'.

I want to thank God for giving me a second chance at redemption, nothing in this life is a coincidence, for he knew my destiny before I was born. He knew all the mistakes I was going to make in order to learn the lessons I needed to in turn inspire women all around the world. I want to thank him for giving me purpose again after many years of living in darkness. I am using this medium to reach out to the many girls and women out there that are stuck, stuck in a vicious cycle of what next? Not knowing who you are, what you want out of life and who to share your fears with. I am reaching out to women who have been subjected to a world of sex, through abuse or for financial freedom, this is a sign that it is never too late to let go and let God take charge of your life, lean on him and trust that he will take you in with no judgement. Life has been unfair to most of us and sometimes we become trapped in a cycle that constantly diminishes our self-worth leaving it in the hands of men who use and abuse us for their selfish desires, but I'm assuring you that you and only you have the power to take back your crown, place it on the top of your head, strap those heels up and walk away from anything or anyone who no longer serves a purpose in our lives. The power lies within you, fight until you change the narrative.

My life was not easy. I made some decisions I regret and am ashamed of, but I own my shit. I own my mistakes, misjudgments and my past. I may not be proud of the way I handled my introduction to sexuality and my past decisions, but I am proud of myself as a flawed and imperfect human. My misadventures cost me so much, my family, my friends, my dignity and reputation at some point and my sense of self. I lost myself to the false promises of happiness hidden within the dollar notes handed to me from one man to another. I believed, truly believed my happiness lied there, subconsciously I believed that these men were giving me something my father couldn't, love and attention, even in its temporary form.

Like I mentioned in the beginning of this book, I wasn't writing this book to explain myself to anyone or seek approval or judgement. I wrote this book to show that I was a flawed and misguided person and that those who feel or can relate to me should know that they are not alone. That I finally found my happiness and acceptance when I learnt to love and be loved. My self-actualization came only after I accepted that the lifestyle I was living was, even though profitable, wasn't sustainable. What I was giving up for it was too costly.

This book was hard to write. I searched within myself, I worked on my mental health and my emotional health as well before I took on this self-assigned project. I want young girls to read this and relate to some, if not all, of my words. This world we live in is only too happy to crush those perceived as weak, I was never weak, my faults and mistakes didn't make me weak, instead it educated me and made me stronger. I hope that girls who have found themselves in similar positions such as myself know that they are not weak, but strong but sometimes it is easy to fall into weakness and weakness can be dangerous. The danger is the comfort and convenience of that lifestyle, knowing that all you have to do is give up a piece of yourself to men who gain perverse pleasure from using you all for money. Knowing when to stop is so much more important. You must want what is best for you. It was after my second pregnancy that I finally knew what I truly wanted in my life; to be a good mother and to be financially dependent on no one but myself, to be a good wife and to love myself.

Finding God, or rather Truly knowing God and realising He was there for me was one of the greatest things to ever happen to me. There are moments of weakness and struggles for me still. There are moments where the guilt weighs me down and I feel rotten and hopeless and unhappy. When I remember that I am not alone, I was never truly alone I am filled with strength and hope and I am filled with forgiveness; for the ones who introduced me to this life, for the ones who didn't do enough to protect me, from the ones who made me feel like it was all my fault and for myself as well who did it all and allowed it all.

The bible, the very book that filled me with hopeless rage after my mother died became my solace and companion. It became my teacher and conscience and it helped me be a good wife, a great mother and a person my son and I can be proud of any day. There is a saying that reads loosely that says your circumstances will, one day, become your redemption story, and that has become my reality. I am a very good example of that. My life went from horrible to this; perfect, amazing and fulfilling. I am surrounded by the people who truly love me despite my flaws and hiccups.

One day you will find it, or maybe you already have. What is important is how you appreciate the honour of living a life as interesting as mine and how you have or will rise from the ashes of your mistakes. You need to love yourself and never entrust anyone one with that. You are the first person you need to forgive and love. You can't say you have a redemption story if you are constantly punishing yourself. Life isn't easy so at least let someone (that someone being you) love you entirely and unconditionally.

Someone once told me you can't choose love and money. It often never works out, you either choose the love of your life, or you choose a man who gives you the comfortable life you could only dream of while lacking the aspect of love. That person was wrong, the question shouldn't have been between Love and Money, instead it should have been Love and Security. I found Love and Security; not just in the man I married but also in myself. I gave myself what I lacked and that was just the start. I married an amazing and ambitious man; I have a gorgeous son and I am happy

A Letter to My Younger Self

Dear baby girl,

Relax! Live in the moment, don't get caught up in the difficulties, their only temporary,

Take life one step at a time, the world is bigger than you think,

Stay in school, knowledge is power,

Be kinder to yourself, don't dwell on the negative but look forth to the positive,

Take a risk, Get out of your comfort zone occasionally,

Don't dwell on what you don't have, appreciate what you do have.

Stop caring about what other people think, focus on the woman you want to become,

Don't be in a rush to grow up, adulthood isn't that great,

Lastly, everything happens for a reason without mistakes you would never learn, without failures you would never achieve greatness, learn to pick yourself up again and keep on striving because "it's not about how many times you fall down, but how many times you get back up"- Abraham Lincoln

ABOUT THE AUTHOR

Born in Houston Texas, wife to an amazing husband and full-time mum to a beautiful baby boy, I have lived a life some would describe as book worthy. I was born in the early '90s in Brooklyn New York before moving to Lagos Nigeria at the age of 11. My name is **Amanda Mukosolu Okpala Adewusi.**

I did not live the typical life a teenager would. My teenage years were filled with a lot of sexual adventures and "bad behaviors". I suffered the devastating loss of my mother when I was 17 and had to deal with an almost non-existent father. I went from being the average teenage girl to dating men who landed me in jail numerous times to sleeping with married men for money and luxury items all in the quest for financial freedom and material things. However, my life changed when I met my husband. He is God-sent. He opened my eyes and helped me realize the life I was living was not worth it. He helped me through the path of salvation. Now, at age 30, I have achieved so much, now a successful businesswoman with several businesses and a mother to a wonderful boy.

This is a story of my path to true freedom and peace. In this book, I tell a story about the mistakes I made in becoming an adult and how I fell into a vicious life of crime and sex for trade. I tell the story of my missteps, my relationship with my parents and how that had an impact on the path I chose. You will read of a girl who needed help but got it from the wrong people and how my desperation and immaturity was exploited by the people who knew better.

I have always loved writing; it is a way of expressing myself. Every time I was depressed and in a dark place, writing was my escape. I started writing as a young girl as a way of expressing my feelings. After I gave my life to Christ and amended my way of life, I knew I had to tell my story. I am a socialite with a lot of influence in the entertainment and movie industry. I also have a large influence on younger girls in Nigeria and this is my way of getting through a larger audience of younger girls.

I want people to learn from my story. I want girls to identify themselves through my story and see what is possible. I want girls to have a renewed mind and restoration through my story. I believe I went through all of these to save someone out there and this is my way of doing that. I wrote this book with the intention of not just sharing my story but also as a cautionary tale for young girls who have chosen to take the same path that I once did; whether due to difficult circumstances or from curiosity. To tell them that they aren't alone, they are understood and that there is a light at the end of the tunnel.

I hope you read my book. learn from it, feel and relate to it. I hope you read it and understand more, and judge less. I hope you become more sympathetic, and more conscientious with your decisions. And I also hope, for those of you that can relate, peace of mind.